born of clay

born of
clay

Ceramics from the
National Museum of the
American Indian

NMAI EDITIONS

NATIONAL MUSEUM OF THE AMERICAN INDIAN

SMITHSONIAN INSTITUTION

The National Museum of the American Indian, Smithsonian Institution, is dedicated to working in collaboration with the indigenous peoples of the Americas to protect and foster Native cultures throughout the Western Hemisphere. The museum's publishing program seeks to augment awareness of Native American beliefs and lifeways, and to educate the public about the history and significance of Native cultures.

Head of Publications, NMAI:
    Terence Winch
Editors: Holly Stewart
    and Amy Pickworth
Designers: Steve Bell
    and Nancy Bratton

First edition
10 9 8 7 6 5 4 3 2

Library of Congress Cataloging-in-Publication Data
Born of clay : ceramics from the National Museum of the American Indian / by Ramiro Matos ... [et al.].— 1st ed.
     p. cm.
"Published in conjunction with the exhibition *Born of Clay: Ceramics from the National Museum of the American Indian*, on view at the National Museum of the American Indian's George Gustav Heye Center in New York, 3 November 2005 through spring 2007."
1. Indian pottery—Exhibitions. 2. Indians—Material culture—Exhibitions. 3. Indians—Antiquities—Exhibitions. 4. Pottery—America—Exhibitions. 5. America—Antiquities—Exhibitions. 6. National Museum of the American Indian (U.S.). George Gustav Heye Center—Exhibitions. I. Matos Mendieta, Ramiro. II. National Museum of the American Indian (U.S.). George Gustav Heye Center.
E59.P8B67 2005
738.089'97—dc22
                    2005029010

Cover: Maya tripod bowl depicting a bird, A.D. 1–650. Campeche, Mexico. Modeled and painted (pre- and postfiring) ceramic, 3.75 by 13.75 in. 24/7762. Photo by Ernest Amoroso.

Late Mississippian globular bottle, A.D. 1450–1600. Rose Place, Cross County, Arkansas. Modeled and incised ceramic, 8.5 by 8.75 in. 17/4224. Photo by Walter Larrimore.

Back Cover: Tiwanaku pedestal-based censer with jaguar, A.D. 600–900. Tiwanaku, Department of La Paz, Bolivia. Modeled and painted ceramic, 11.25 by 12 in. 20/6313. Photo by Ernest Amoroso.

Half title page: Dora Cook Bradby (Pamunkey) finishing the rim of a pot, ca. 1980. King William, Virginia. Photo by Chip Clark. Courtesy of Warren Cook, Assistant Chief, Pamunkey Tribal Government.

Title Page: Tile masks, ca. 2002. Made by Nora Naranjo-Morse (Santa Clara, b. 1953). Santa Clara Pueblo, New Mexico. Modeled and painted ceramic, largest: 7.75 by 4 in. 26/5270. Photo by Walter Larrimore.

For information about the National Museum of the American Indian, visit the NMAI website at www.AmericanIndian.si.edu.

Contents

Foreword
Born of Clay

WHAT WE CALL CLAY is actually a kind of mineral deposit. The composition of a lump of clay depends on where it was harvested: it is a true reflection of the land it was drawn from, a revelation of its history. Clay is created by an immensely slow process, something akin to rock + water + eons. When we add fire to this equation, we have ceramic—durable, profoundly useful, and for many Native peoples, an important means of creative expression. Many of our most exceptional objects are born of clay that—like ourselves—was born of our homelands, and from the deep histories they contain.

In 2010, as part of the National Museum of the American Indian's Renewing Connections project, artist Nora Naranjo-Morse (Santa Clara) participated in a residency at the Center for Indigenous Arts in El Tajín, Veracruz, Mexico, with her daughter, Eliza. Describing the experience in an interview, she said, "At any given moment, I would hear several languages being spoken around the table, yet the universal language that connected us was the clay." Naranjo-Morse added that this scene, centered on a table crowded with women working in clay, was similar to many she remembered from her own childhood in New Mexico. There's something very beautiful in how this image addresses both the social aspect of creation and the ways in which we pass on cultural traditions.

That work in clay can transcend language, time, and place is something we observe time and again as we study our collections. The National Museum of the American Indian (NMAI) is honored to serve as the steward of an extraordinary ceramics collection; it includes some 60,000 pieces spanning more than 6,000 years of Native life in the Western Hemisphere. More than ninety percent of these objects are complete, a fact that sets our holdings apart from any other collection of similar size and scope. *Born of Clay* highlights some of these remarkable works.

Since this book was first published in 2005, access to the museum's collections has increased dramatically through a searchable database available on our website, www.AmericanIndian.si.edu. Our alliances with communities and tribal museums in Central and South America have grown and deepened. NMAI has established an Office for Latin America, headed by the esteemed scholar José Barreiro (Taíno). As much of this book showcases the ceramics of Mesoamerican and South America, we have released it in a Spanish-language version, making it more accessible to individuals, scholars, and—most importantly—the indigenous communities where so many of these vessels were created. NMAI has also teamed up with the Smithsonian Latino Center on the Central American Ceramics Research Project, a special initiative to study, document, and identify items in our Central American ceramics collections.

The circumstances surrounding the exhibition *Born of Clay*, which was on view in New York at the National Museum of the American Indian's location in Lower Manhattan between November 5, 2005, and May 20, 2007, and the original publication of the book remain the same as they were seven years ago; with some minor updates, I include here the acknowledgments offered by my predecessor, W. Richard West, Jr. (Southern Cheyenne). To these I add my own special thanks to Tim Johnson (Mohawk), associate director for museum programs, and Tanya Thrasher (Cherokee), publications manager, under whose leadership both this revision and the Spanish-language edition came into being.

The museum is grateful to artists Exaltación Mamani Amaro (Quechua), Jody Folwell (Santa Clara), Peter B. Jones (Onondaga), Rubén Agurio Martínez Martínez (Nahua), Irma Rodríguez Moroco (Quechua), Al Qöyawayma (Hopi), Eleazar Navarrete Ramírez (Nahua), and Jereldine Redcorn (Caddo/ Potawatomi) for the wealth of knowledge and imagination they have brought to our understanding of ceramics techniques and potters' creative processes.

We also remain deeply indebted to the late Felipe Solís, who was the director of the National Museum of Anthropology in Mexico City, for graciously curating NMAI's Mesoamerican collections for this project. The scholarship of Ann McMullen, Thomas E. Evans (Pawnee), Patricia L. Nietfeld, Ramiro Matos (Quechua), and former assistant director Bruce Bernstein are reflected throughout this book. Thanks are due as well to curatorial assistants Theresa Burchett-Anderson, Paz Núñez Regueiro, and Verónica Velasquez Sánchez-Hidalgo, and to Carmen Arellano (Tarma Quechua), Warren Cook (Pamunkey), Uriel Orellana (Chortí Maya), and Carlos Quiroz (Muchik) for their contributions to our knowledge of our collections. John Haworth (Cherokee), director of the NMAI's exhibition space in Lower Manhattan, contributed in countless ways to the success of *Born of Clay.*

Machel Monenerkit (Comanche) was the project manager for the exhibition. Veronica Jenkins Harrell and Bob Mastrangelo provided administrative support. Gerry Breen designed the gallery spaces, with Peter Brill. Kate Mitchell edited the exhibition text. Deborah Alden, Sooja Lee, and Susanna Stieff created the exhibition graphics. Stacey Jones led the installation team. Emily Kaplan and Megan Emery coordinated conservation of the ceramics collections, with Marian Kaminitz and a team of conservators. Collections management staff Fran Biehl Felber, Dominique Cocuzza, Robert Marvin Garcia Hunt, and Tony Williams were responsible for the care of the objects. Rajshree Solanki served as registrar. Johanna Gorelick conceived of the educational programs that complemented the project. Lucia DeRespinis, Trey Moynihan, Jihan Robinson, and Ann Marie Sekeres led the development effort.

The beautiful object photographs in this book are the work of the NMAI photo services staff, under the direction of Cynthia Frankenburg, including photographers Ernest Amoroso, Walter Larrimore, and Roger Whiteside, and digital technician William Greene. Additional object images were taken by the NMAI move team under the direction of Scott Merritt. This book would not have been produced without the commitment of the museum's publications office, especially Terence Winch, former head of publications, and Ann Kawasaki. Steve Bell created the lively design of these pages, assisted by Nancy Bratton. Holly Stewart and Amy Pickworth edited the text. We are especially grateful for the support of the late Lou Stancari, NMAI photo archivist, who aided the archival photo research for the exhibition and tirelessly supported the project from its inception. We respectfully dedicate this book to our beloved colleague Lou and his enduring legacy at the museum. Finally, we wish to thank Barbara and James Block for their support of the exhibition *Born of Clay,* and Dr. Richard Mansfield for his generous donation of Southwest pottery to our collections.

—Kevin Gover (Pawnee)
Director, National Museum of the American Indian

Introduction
Cultural Continuity

I FIRST ENCOUNTERED NATIVE AMERICAN CERAMICS along old U.S. Route 66. I was ten, and traveling from western Oklahoma to Southern California with my cousin Jerald and my parents. This was in the early 1960s, decades before I'd ever heard the phrases "cultural tourism" and "destination marketing," the promotional lingo used by museums looking for ways to reach new audiences, promote our programs and exhibitions, and join forces with other cultural institutions. As we drove west across New Mexico, there were Native artisans on the roadside selling their work, as well as rows upon rows of pots for sale in gas stations, rest stops, and motel lobbies. For the next few hundred miles there were pots everywhere! We were en route to Disney's Magic Kingdom, but along the way, on this family journey, we passed through a world that proved far more marvelous, and has remained much more vivid in my memory.

Given the depth, breadth, and sheer volume of the ceramic treasures of the National Museum of the American Indian, it seems curious that we are only now, more than a decade after NMAI opened its location in New York, getting around to presenting this survey. Certainly, *Born of Clay* does not represent the frst time ceramics from our permanent collections have been prominently on view at NMAI-NY or in the new museum on the National Mall in Washington, D.C. The contemporary cera-mist Rina Swentzell (Tewa/Santa Clara) was one of twenty-three Native selectors who chose works of art and cultural expression from the collections for the exhibition *All Roads Are Good: Native Voices on Life and Culture,* which marked the opening of NMAI-NY in 1994.

From her perspective as a potter, Rina recognized a remarkable, energetic power of design and form in the objects she selected. She described the profound sense of spontaneity and play embedded in Native ceramics, exemplified today in her own work; how the act of making a pot always involves a social gathering; and how, for many Native people, pottery-making and other creative work is simply part of everyday life. Rina appreciated the superb aesthetic quality of the ceramics she chose, but she also wanted people to be aware of the spiritual significance of ceramics, expressed in the depictions of living beings—human, animal, and plant—on the pots, and manifest in pottery's deep connection to Native communities. After all, the material to make pottery comes from the earth itself. The art form is literally grounded in the potter's homeland.

In light of that fact, the museum recently invited contemporary Native potters Exaltación Mamani Amaro (Quechua), Jody Folwell (Santa Clara), Peter B. Jones (Onondaga), Rubén Agurio Martínez Martínez (Nahua), Irma Rodríguez Moroco (Quechua), Al Qöyawayma (Hopi), Eleazar Navarrete

Ramírez (Nahua), and Jereldine Redcorn (Caddo/ Potawatomi) to join Felipe Solís, director of the National Museum of Anthropology in Mexico City, and our own curatorial staff in selecting and interpreting some of the most remarkable pieces from the museum's extraordinary ceramics collections. In this book and the accompanying exhibition, the insights of these Native artists, representing the living Native communities of the Andes, the eastern United States, Mexico, and the American Southwest, complement the curatorial overviews of their ceramic traditions. Together, they tell a fascinating story of cultural continuity.

To give one example of this continuity: contemporary cultural historians, artists, and critics—Native and non-Native—have pointed out that the exchange between Native potters and those who buy their work is complex, driven by multiple motives on both sides. *Born of Clay* makes clear that this dynamic is hardly new. Whether we are considering the ancient Olmec trade in straight-sided tripod vessels, elite versus traditional aesthetics in the Mississippian world, or the appeal of Southwest-ern art and culture that still fuels roadside pottery stands, the market has always influenced what potters make. Similarly, artists have always been driven by the need to support their families and communities, but also by their own vision, by the challenge of technical and aesthetic innovation, and by the tactile and spiritual pleasure of making something new and lasting from the earth's clay.

In the years since *All Roads,* NMAI-NY has presented ceramic art by Arthur Amiotte (Oglala Lakota), Nora Naranjo-Morse (Santa Clara), Anita Fields (Osage/Creek), and Virgil Ortiz (Cochiti), among others, as well as treasures from contemporary Mexico and from the collection of Charles and Valerie Diker. I hope this new book and exhibition, introducing some of the most thought-provoking pieces from our collections, will lead to even wider public appreciation for Native potters and pottery, and will inspire further scholarship about this most lasting of the human arts.

—JOHN HAWORTH (Cherokee)
Director of NMAI-NY

RAMIRO MATOS

The Andes
Embracing Tradition

SCHOLARS SOMETIMES REFER TO CERAMICS as "the book of Andean cultural history," for pottery is the principal source of our understanding of the societies that rose in the mountain peaks and river valleys of present-day western South America. The high quality and great variety of pottery found throughout the Andes, classified by date, style, and location, has enabled archaeologists to define distinct cultural areas within the region and to construct cultural chronologies of its history. So central is the ceramic record to our understanding of this world that the early history of the region is divided into the Preceramic and Ceramic periods. No evidence has been found, however, of the possible invention of ceramics in the Americas. Rather, the craft of pottery-making simply appears within the same archaic cultures that developed early agriculture and textiles woven from plant and animal fibers.

The oldest ceramics known in the Americas, made between 5,000 and 6,000 years ago, are found along the Pacific Coast of present-day Ecuador, at Valdivia and Puerto Hormiga, and in the San Jacinto Valley of Colombia. In Peru, at Yarinacocha and Wairajirca, objects between 3,800 and 4,000 years old have been recovered. From these locations the production of ceramics spread throughout the Andean cultural area. Some archaeologists believe ceramics technology was also carried by sea to Mesoamerica, the second great cradle of civilization in the Americas. The appeal of ceramic technology is no mystery. Ceramics are one of the best answers to the needs of civilizations, from the demands of domestic life to the observance of public and religious activities.

The earliest Andean ceramics appear to have been associated with temples, pastoral–agricultural economies, and a very complex society that had established priesthoods and centralized political power. This pottery is extremely beautiful, often of black and brown color, almost baroque, with decorations made by embossing, incising, rocker-stamping, or burnishing. The best-developed styles found in the central and southern Andes are the ceramics found near the ceremonial site at Chavín de Huántar (800–400 B.C.) and Cupisnique (1000–400 B.C.).

Tiwanaku pedestal-based censer with condor, A.D. 600–900. Tiwanaku, Department of La Paz, Bolivia. Molded and painted ceramic, 10.5 by 13.5 in. 24/4450

The ceramics of these two societies represent divine entities, often shown with feline faces, condor feathers, or the heads of snakes. The predominant shapes were bottles with bracket handles, round pots, and fine sculptures of humans, plants, and animals.

During the same period, another culture developed on the southern coast of Peru, in the area called Paracas. The Paracas culture (600–100 B.C.) produced marvelous works of embossed ceramic finished with a thick oil applied after firing. Paracas is also known for its brilliant embroidered fabrics, which remain intact today. This colorful tradition in ceramics and textiles was followed by the Nazca culture (A.D. 1–600), whose potters developed improved techniques for preparing clay and for decorating objects, using fine brushes to paint sophisticated motifs. In the early stage of Nazca ceramics, potters painted realistic characters and landscapes. In later periods they represented abstract shapes that are difficult to interpret. Nazca drawings show characters with mixed realistic and mythological features. The carnivore whale, centipede, evil cat, octopus, and other icons were part of Nazca cosmology, probably representing symbols of supernatural power.

While the polychrome style was preferred along the southern coast of Peru, the Moche cultures (A.D. 1–800) that flourished on the northern coast produced extraordinary clay sculptures and effigies decorated with fine lines of red on a beige background. Moche artists also developed the ceramic technique of modeling. Their pottery stands out for its *huacos retrato* (portrait vases), works on which human faces are shown expressing different emotions—happiness, sadness, anger, melancholy—as well for its complicated drawings of wars, human sacrifices, and celebrations. Farther north the Vicús culture (A.D. 1–500) made remarkable ceramics with decorations done in negative/positive technique using red and white pigments. The Vicús people also made beautiful figures representing plants and animals, and people hunting, fishing, healing the sick, or seated engaging in some other activity.

A similar cultural evolution took place in Ecuador during the same period. Ceramics created by the Machalilla (1500–500 B.C.) and Chorrera (1000–1 B.C.) cultures mark the close of the Formative period, which began at Valdivia, and the opening of the period called Regional Development (A.D. 1–1000). During this period, new styles emerged from the Guangala (A.D. 100–900), Jama Coaque (200 B.C.–A.D. 600), and Bahía (200 B.C.–A.D. 600) cultures as well. The art of these societies is best known for representations of human and animal figures,

Cupisnique snake-shaped, stirrup-spout bottle, 500–100 B.C. Tembladera, Department of Cajamarca, Peru. Modeled and incised ceramic, 8 by 6.75 in. 24/3535

Animals were created by the Machulas (ancestor spirits). Birds carry messages to the spirits. Felines—the *uturunku* (jaguar) and *osqollu* (ocelot)—rule the mountains. In thanks for the llama and other domestic animals, we make offerings to Pachamama (Mother Earth), the Wamanis (mountain spirits), and the Machulas several times each year.

In pottery, our ancestors portrayed the three levels in the Andean conception of the world: the condor represents the sky world; the puma, the earth; and the snake, the underworld. In other ways, vessels with three parts may have been used to hold offerings: wine to the earth, *chicha* (maize beer) to the sky, and water to the underworld.

—Exaltación Mamani Amaro (Quechua) and Irma Rodríguez Moroco (Quechua)

Paracas feline-shaped, bridge-handle bottle, 400–200 B.C. Cahuachi, Department of Ica, Peru. Modeled, incised, and painted ceramic, 6 by 9 in. 23/8375

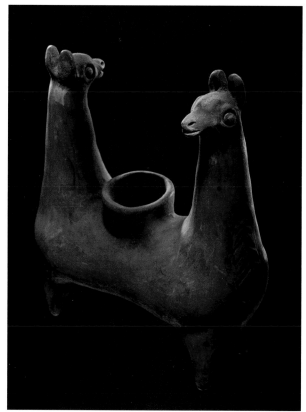

Quechua two-headed llama, 2005. Raqchi, Department of Cusco, Peru. Modeled ceramic, 6.5 by 6.5 in. 26/5356

Moche toad-shaped, stirrup-spout bottle, A.D. 1–200. Northern coast of Peru. Modeled and painted ceramic, 6.5 by 7.5 in. 23/6189

Tiwanaku bottle depicting Wiraqocha
(the staff god), A.D. 700–1300. Peru.
Modeled and painted ceramic, 7.25
by 5 in. 23/6464

Inka *paqcha* (ritual vessel) depicting
a llama head with *arybalo* (jar) on
top, A.D. 1500–1600. Department of
Cusco, Peru. Modeled and painted
ceramic, 8 by 9 in. 16/4835

which were made in molds. Jama Coaque and Bahía figurines are both simplistic and elaborately iconographic. Particular subjects of interest include characters performing specific tasks: musicians playing instruments, priests and shamans officiating, or warriors and royalty, often shown displaying their prizes.

The Nazca, Moche, Vicús, and Recuay (A.D. 100–800) in Peru, and the Guangala, Jama Coaque, and Bahía in Ecuador, are referred to as the "Master Craftsmen," the people of these societies achieved such impressive levels of technical and artistic creativity. The beauty of their ceramics is reflected not only in the quality of the modeling, but also in the complexity of the designs. The Recuay people also knew how to use fine, white kaolin clay.

After the collapse of this period, two political–religious movements, known as Wari (A.D. 500–900) and Tiwanaku (A.D. 400–800), rose in the central and southern Andean regions. Both societies were well-organized states. Despite their unstable politics, these states managed to establish official styles for pottery, both in form and iconography. Standardized ceramic shapes and designs from this period are found in different sites, though with local variations. The decoration is polychrome, and there is an obsession with representing the human face in the neck of the vases. The main motif is the god Wiraqocha, a deity with human features believed to be a later incarnation of the god depicted in Chavín stone stelae. Animals, including the puma or jaguar, condor, and snake, also served as sources of ceramic designs, sometimes painted and sometimes modeled.

After the fall of these Andean movements, many regional kingdoms appeared, among them the Chimú (A.D. 800–1400) on the northern coast of Peru; Chuquibamba (A.D. 100-1400) in the southern Andes (in what is today Arequipa,

Peru); and the Tuza (A.D. 1000–1500), Piartal (A.D. 1000–1500), Panzaleo (A.D. 900–1500), and Manteño (A.D. 500–1500) in Ecuador. These kingdoms produced great numbers of ceramic objects, often made with patterns or molds. The decoration of these pieces is predominantly geometric and monochrome, but they lack the artistic quality of earlier cultures' work.

During the second half of the fifteenth century, a new political force developed in the Andes. This civilization originated in Cusco and conquered, militarily and culturally, the territory of present-day Colombia, Ecuador, Peru, and Bolivia; half of Chile; and the northwestern corner of Argentina. This was the empire of the Tawantinsuyu, governed by the Inka kings, who were considered by their people to be the sons of the Inti (sun) god. Inka officials regulated both education and religion. The economy, too, was strictly organized and controlled by the state. The production of pottery was standardized. Its shapes, decorations, and even its uses were decided by the state. At the local level, regional pottery was still made, and these ceramics show the influence of local traditions and styles of decoration. Yet *arybalos* (bottles with bridge handles), plates, *qochas* (chambered vessels), and *paqchas* (vessels used to make offerings) all belonged to a class of imperial property associated with social and religious ceremonies.

Despite the Spanish conquest, many pre-Columbian traditions survived through the colonial era and continue to be observed. Andean ceramics technology has changed very little during the last 500 years.

Wari double-spout-and-bridge bottle depicting condors, A.D. 800–1000. Doña María, central coast of Peru. Modeled and painted ceramic, 5.5 by 7.75 in. 24/3817

The ceramics selected to be shown here include objects from different cultures and sites, and from the earliest times to today. The museum particularly wishes to recognize two contemporary Quechua ceramists from Raqchi, a community located next to the palace of Wiraqocha in Cusco, Peru, who shared with us their traditions and knowledge: Exaltación Mamani Amaro and Irma Rodríguez Moroco. During our discussions, Exaltación and Irma expressed a vision of the ceramics of the Andes that is very different from this archaeological account. They were not concerned with the historic cultural relationships among objects in the museum's collections, or with their style. Instead, they classified objects by their use. It was easy, for example, to recognize the *siku* (pipe flute), as well as the paqchas and qochas. In the case of figures, Exaltación and Irma identified the animals and their associations within Andean cosmology.

From our conversations it emerged that, regardless of the differences that distinguish pre-Columbian ceramics, pottery-making follows a common tradition and shares similarities: in techniques of modeling and firing, in shapes related to their function, and in certain decorative criteria. Despite the changes that

Left: Lidded bowl with puma handles, 2005. Made by Exaltación Mamani Amaro (Quechua, b. 1962) and Irma Rodríguez Moroco (Quechua, b. 1969). Raqchi, Department of Cusco, Peru. Modeled and painted ceramic, 2 by 3.5 in. 26/5291

Right: *Qero* **(ritual vessel),** 2005. Made by Exaltación Mamani Amaro (Quechua, b. 1962) and Irma Rodríguez Moroco (Quechua, b. 1969). Raqchi, Department of Cusco, Peru. Modeled and painted ceramic, 2.5 by 3.25 in. 26/5293

OUR HERITAGE

In our community, Raqchi, we are trying hard to preserve our Inka heritage.

Our people have always been potters. In our language, *raqchi* means "pottery." Our techniques have come down to us through our parents. Our materials are clay, water, and fire, and all of these things are alive. Pachamama gives all and feeds all. Pottery is made from her body.

—Exaltación Mamani Amaro (Quechua)

Quechua jar, 2005. Raqchi, Department of Cusco, Peru. Modeled and painted ceramic, 12 by 7.5 in. 26/5351

have occurred in the production of pottery due to the widespread availability of plastic goods and the pressures of modern western society, contemporary indigenous potters have kept their knowledge and practice of traditional technology as well as their cosmological vision.

To the potters of Raqchi, clay is the child of the Pachamama (Mother Earth). "Our materials are clay, water, and fire, and all of these things are alive. Pachamama gives all and feeds all. Pottery is made from her body," Exaltación explains. In the potters' worldview, clay is family and pottery objects are our brothers and sisters. Communities recognize the technical skill of potters, who are considered to be protected by the spirits for their ability to transform clay into objects useful in religious observance and everyday life. Through ceramics the potter expresses ideas and values. Clay records the metaphors and symbols that animate the imagination of the people. Potters take some of their imagery from the world around them; other images are copied from Inka and pre-Inka models. Potters believe that copying the old models evokes the past and enables them to re-encounter their ancestors.

The ceramists use a language and iconography related to production. This form of communication encompasses both the traditional and contemporary worlds, the latter the world of tourists' demands. Today, some objects are made for domestic use, some for use in rituals, but most are made to be sold in the commercial market. New forms and shapes adopted to appeal to tourists have become integrated into contemporary indigenous rituals and cosmological views. Potters appreciate the contribution tourism makes to their families' lives, and the opportunity to take part in the commercial economy and share aspects of their cultural heritage. As Irma explains, "When we produce pottery for the market, we try to follow our parents' and grandparents' ways. But this is changing, and I try to incorporate my surroundings, including the tourists, into my work."

The two main techniques for constructing or forming ceramics are coiling and pinching, and to these are added modeling, or hand-forming, and the use of molds. The indigenous pottery of the Andes is now also made using the *torno* (wheel). Potters usually fire their work in open ovens, though they use closed ovens for certain special pieces. Objects destined for commercial use are fired in open ovens at a temperature of 600 degrees centigrade. Larger pieces for domestic use are fired in closed ovens at temperatures of 900 to 1000 degrees centigrade. When a potter makes an object for ritual use, he or she pays special attention to the selection of the clay and to its firing.

The potters of Raqchi, says Exaltación, "guide their work with the strength of their beliefs and with the technique inherent in the material. We inherited both from our ancestors." Cosmology can exercise a strong conservative influence on contemporary ceramics. Yet potters also operate within a realm of interactions controlled by physical and chemical laws, and within a framework of modern economic, aesthetic, and technical choices that must be re-evaluated constantly.

"The clay allows us to transmit our knowledge and our desires. Here we have pieces that symbolize our Quechua cosmology, with its complementary forces of male and female, positive and negative. Through these pieces, we can hear the messages our grandparents left for us, and when we use the same designs, we project them into the future."

—Exaltación Mamani Amaro (Quechua)

ANN MCMULLEN, THOMAS E. EVANS, AND PATRICIA L. NIETFELD

Rivers of Interaction
Ceramics of Eastern North America

IN NATIVE NORTH AMERICA, the broad areas east of the Great Plains share history and lifeways that differentiate them from other parts of the continent. For ceramics, this is especially true, since ceramics' roots in the East long precede those of the better-known pottery of the American Southwest. This essay provides a brief background and context for appreciating Native pottery of the Northern and Southern Woodlands—from the Great Lakes and Oklahoma eastward, including Maritime Canada, and south to Florida—and the people who have produced it over the last 4,500 years.

Beginnings

Eastern North America's earliest documented pottery was made along the coast of present-day Georgia about 2500 B.C., and the manufacture of pottery spread through the Southeast over the next 500 years. Throughout the East, ceramics predate agriculture, and the advent of pottery generally signals the transition from hunter-gatherer lifeways of what is called the Archaic period (beginning around 6000 B.C.) to the Woodland period (which began as early as 1200 B.C. in the South), when larger and increasingly sedentary populations relied on agriculture.

From these beginnings, pottery spread up the Mississippi River, reaching the Ohio River Valley by about 1100 B.C. and Wisconsin by 500 B.C. While all pottery in eastern North America is assumed to stem from its Georgia origins, its spread did not necessarily entail one person teaching another. Instead, the *idea* of mixing clay with temper—such as sand, crushed rock, or grass—and firing it to create durable vessels seems to have been passed along, yielding different ceramic technologies and forms. By 1000 B.C., ceramics had spread north to Delaware, and to New York and southern Ontario by 600 B.C. The expansion of pottery—and perhaps that of agriculture—through the East was fostered by widespread trade networks exchanging copper from the Great Lakes; shell from the Gulf of Mexico; and mica, pigments, quartz crystals, and exotic lithic materials from

Middle Woodland (Deptford culture) jar, 100 B.C.–A.D. 100. Hall Mound, Wakulla County, Florida. Modeled, incised, and painted ceramic, 8.75 by 4.5 in. 17/3982

other areas. The myriad waterways of the Mississippi River drainage system were the primary infrastructure of these trade and interaction networks.

Ultimately, eastern ceramics shared basic technological and decorative principles: clay mixed with temper was coiled and smoothed with a paddle or a scraper to form pots with pointed or rounded bases that could be set in soft earth or propped over a fire. While the clay was still damp, the sides of the pots were pressed with soft textiles or sticks wrapped with cord, or incised with decorative lines. Archaeologists can use a vessel's shape, technological characteristics, and designs to identify its style and thus link it with a specific people and time period.

Form, Function, and Use

For thousands of years, eastern Native people carried and stored water in hide bags or wooden or bark vessels. Meat, fish, and other foods were cooked over open fires or "stone boiled" by dropping heated stones into non-ceramic containers holding food and water or some other liquid. Dried meat or shellfish could be rehydrated and cooked more easily in pots, as could wild seeds and vegetables. As agriculture became established, many foods were dried for later use, and Native potters developed forms suited to the long cooking times of dried corn and beans.

Although many later potters made highly decorated special-purpose ceramics, production of cooking vessels was the earliest and most continuous impetus for pottery-making. According to European explorers' accounts, women produced most Native pottery in the East. Beyond its use for cooking, pottery served other purposes, and had other meanings. Pots of food and water were buried with the dead to provide their spirits with sustenance during the journey to the hereafter. Where Native people cremated their dead, fine pots were used to inter the deceased's ashes. In making ceramics for specific purposes—whether feeding one's family, burying a loved one, or for ceremonial use—Native potters worked their honor and devotion into the clay.

Trading in Ideas

The Archaic period trade networks that led to the spread of ceramics also heralded the beginning of other broad social and cultural changes. About 4,000 years ago, southeastern societies built their first earthworks and mounds, a tradition that grew over the next 3,500 years to reach from Oklahoma to New York and Wisconsin to Florida. Interest in eastern moundbuilding cultures has been profound, and much is known about Native lifeways during this deep timespan.

During the Archaic period, Native people adapted to increasingly settled lifestyles, taking advantage of plants, animals, and other natural resources. No single change marked the far-reaching transition from the Archaic to the succeeding Woodland period, starting about 3,200 years ago in the South and about 1,000 years ago in northern areas. Instead, a series of inventions and ideas arose and expanded, leading to larger changes throughout the entire area. These included use of bows and arrows rather than spears; increasing dependence on corn, beans, squash, and other agricultural produce; the establishment of more permanent villages; greater variation and elaboration in ceramics, textiles and basketry, leatherwork, and woodwork; the observance of more elaborate funerary rituals; and greater differentiation in individual status.

THE DEPTFORD CULTURE: A HINT OF THINGS TO COME

The large Mississippian sites of the Southeast were centers of powerful warlike chiefdoms. But the highly stratified societies these sites evince, and the sophisticated ceramics they contain, didn't arise overnight. What went before them?

The Deptford culture of coastal South Carolina, Georgia, and northern Florida gives us a glimpse of earlier Woodland period lifeways. Developing out of mobile hunting and gathering populations, the Deptford culture, beginning about 500 B.C., is the first regional culture in this area identifiable by its ceramics, which were tempered with sand and compacted with paddles—technological innovations that produced substantial vessels that could be used for storing food and cooking.

Deptford people made intensive use of the shellfish and fish of the salt marshes and tidal streams beside which they lived, so although they probably did not cultivate plants, their population increased, and they established villages of perhaps five to ten related families led by a respected elder. They also developed trading networks with Hopewell peoples to the north and west, exchanging ornaments made of their local shells for nonlocal copper and stone objects, thereby laying the groundwork for things to come. Pierce, Hall, and other Late Deptford (100 B.C.— A.D. 250) sites located at the bend in the Florida panhandle show evidence of this increased external interaction and the fledgling social and religious complexity it engendered.

The Pierce and Hall sites contain burial mounds, suggesting that some Deptford villages became small ceremonial centers associated with specific social groups and their religious leaders who oversaw mound building and burial rituals. The ceramics associated with these mounds often feature unusual shapes and decoration and are different from vessels found in other Late Deptford villages. These vessels were specially made for ceremonial use, and their burial with certain individuals hints that social stratification had begun. —P.L.N.

Middle Woodland (Deptford culture) jar, 100 B.C.—A.D. 100. Hall Mound, Wakulla County, Florida. Modeled, incised, and painted ceramic, 8.75 by 4.5 in. 17/3982

Within hunting and gathering societies, such as those of the Archaic period, an individual's status often depended on age, gender, and personal accomplishments. Over time, some aspects of personal status were passed down within families or clans, including chiefly lines of descent or hereditary priesthoods. Individuals who controlled valuable trading relationships also gained status through their exclusive access to high-grade raw materials for making stone tools, or shells from distant places that could be made into beads and ornaments. Essentially, differential access to goods and information led to greater or lesser status, and this is often most apparent archaeologically through comparison of grave goods buried with different individuals.

DUCKS AND PRIESTS

In much of the East, Native cosmologies had three basic levels: the Underworld, the Terrestrial World, and the Upper or Sky World. Animals with the power to function across these worlds—such as water birds that could fly into the heavens, walk and nest on land, and dive in the waters of the Underworld and return—were especially venerated. Like water birds, Native shamans and priests also mediated between the worlds. In the Mississippian Southeast, ducks often symbolized the priesthood.

In addition to the supernatural Underwater Panther and the Great Winged Serpent, Mississippian iconography included a crested duck-like animal, most often represented on stone and ceramic bowls as riding the watery waves of the Underworld. Its crest symbolizes the mythical figure of Morning Star and thus the masculine warrior spirit. In combination, symbols of the priesthood and Morning Star may represent a very powerful mythical warrior-priest. —T.E.E.

Late Mississippian bowl depicting a mythical bird, A.D. 1350–1550. Sawyers Landing, Arkansas County, Arkansas. Modeled and incised ceramic, 6.5 by 10.25 in. 17/4167

Late Mississippian bowl depicting a wood duck, A.D. 1300–1500. Stewart County, Tennessee. Modeled ceramic, 5.25 by 9.5 in. 8/2537

During the Woodland period, construction of earthworks and mounds grew, giving rise to cultural expressions such as the Adena complex in the Ohio River Valley approximately 2,500 years ago. Some mounds include the burial sites of high-status individuals who were interred with fine tools, ornaments, and ritual items, many of which originated in distant areas and indicate extensive trade networks in raw materials or finished works of art. A subsequent cultural expression—that of the Hopewell people—spread over a larger area and included even more dramatic earthworks, art, and interaction networks. Through these river-based networks, ideas about ritual, status, technology, and other aspects of culture flowed, creating broad similarities over large regions as well as distinctive localized expressions. Over time, interaction networks often seemed to function through larger population and trade centers at the confluence of large rivers, indicating use of the rivers as trading highways.

The Mississippian period began between A.D. 850 and 1000 and ended between 1500 and 1700 with the arrival of Europeans. The use of ground shell in ceramics, the creation of distinctive art and rectangular mounds, and the observance of intensive ceremonial life based on temples and the veneration of honored ancestors are marks of Mississippian culture, which covered most of the area under consideration here with the exception of New England, New York, and coastal areas where Woodland lifeways persisted. Mississippian societies operated as chiefdoms: paramount chiefs regulated the distribution of food and other goods between urban centers and the outlying farms and settlements that supported the dense populations of these Native cities. Focused at major mound sites such as Cahokia (Illinois), Moundville (Alabama), Etowah (Georgia), Emerald (Mississippi), and Spiro (Oklahoma), paramount chiefs controlled exchanges within their own chiefdoms, with other chiefdoms, and with outlying communities headed by lesser chiefs. Because paramount chiefs took in food and other goods and redistributed them, they could support full-time artists, priests, and other specialized workers.

Mississippian peoples' elaborate pottery is a testament to these artists, who were probably able to focus exclusively on making ceramics. Artists essentially in the employ of the chief or his family could be called upon to create very special works for use in the chief's home, in ceremonies, for the funerals of chiefly individuals and members of their families, or for trade to other high-ranking individuals.

Symbols, signs, and meanings

Widespread eastern trade, interaction networks, and intermarriage between cultural groups created a broad basis of shared designs which are thought to represent shared ideological and ceremonial systems. Some designs were specific to particular regions and times and may have been adapted by others without carrying the same meaning. Over many decades, scholars have attempted to identify these symbols' meanings based on information collected when Europeans first arrived

"These pieces tell about the rituals, the traditions, and the daily lives of the people and how they saw their worlds. In them, I can see our dances, our connection to the lands we were removed from, and I am reminded of the hardships of the people—what they went through to keep our traditions alive."

—Jereldine Redcorn (Caddo/ Potawatomi)

The Southeast's largest and most impressive ceremonial center was Moundville (A.D. 1100–1600), located on the Black Warrior River in west-central Alabama. Wooden palisades enclosed roughly 185 acres, containing residential areas for about 1,000 people and at least thirty mounds surrounding an open plaza. The mounds, topped by wooden religious buildings or elite houses, were arranged in opposing ranked pairs, suggesting that they were associated with the site's ruling clans and purposefully mirrored the sociopolitical stratification characteristic of late Mississippian society.[4]

Until 1300, Moundville was the center of a powerful chiefdom, to which smaller mound centers were subservient. Its influence was wide, as ceramics either made at Moundville or copying typical Moundville motifs are found as far away as Kentucky and Indiana, and pots probably made in Illinois have been excavated at Moundville.

After 1300, many of Moundville's inhabitants seem to have departed, leaving perhaps only ritual specialists, and the site functioned as the necropolis for the surrounding region, with elaborate single burials placed in the mounds and cemeteries taking over former residential areas. Motifs typical of Moundville objects, such as the hand-and-eye, swastika, hand and arm bones, skulls, moth antennae, Winged Serpent, and Underwater Panther, are thought to have associations with death, suggesting that Moundville uniquely functioned as a gateway to the Underworld. —P.L.N.

Late Mississippian bottle with moth antenna design, A.D. 1300–1500. Moundville site, Hale County, Alabama. Modeled and painted ceramic, 8 by 6.25 in. 17/1432

Late Mississippian bottle with raised hand and arm bones, A.D. 1350–1500. Hickman County, Kentucky. Modeled and appliquéd ceramic, 7.5 by 8 in. 4/8063

or by comparison with information about similar designs provided by historic and contemporary Native people. Much of this interpretive effort has focused on Mississippian iconography, because it most clearly relates to information from historic and contemporary Native people.

Archaeologists have pondered what has been called the Southern Cult or the Southeastern Ceremonial Complex—a body of object types, iconography, rituals, and ceremonies shared by Mississippian peoples at the largest mound cities. Depictions of supernatural beings, leaders, warriors, and priests figure strongly, as do rituals surrounding treatment and care of the remains of leading individuals, whose bones were kept in temples built atop flat-topped pyramidal mounds. Southeastern Ceremonial Complex iconography may refer only to the lives of the elite. At the same time, ancient and traditional beliefs about the powers of the universe, the four winds, water, and fertility continued to be held by those who were not part of the elite and who made ceramics and other items for their own use.[5] These designs are often abstract, and their meanings cannot be read directly. Other designs, such as animals, may appear to be representational but undoubtedly also carry other, less apparent, meanings.

In recent years, scholars have delved more deeply into Native oral traditions of the Plains and Southeast to link Mississippian iconography to stories of Morning Star, Evening Star, Red Horn, Underwater Panther, and the Great Winged Serpent.[6] These promising studies provide new ways to think about objects, designs, and the people who used them. While none of this is definitive, the continuing significance of these Native traditions hints at the power these concepts held.

Yesterday, Today, and Tomorrow

The arrival of Europeans spelled the end of much of what had gone before. By the late fifteenth century, Basque and English fishermen explored the shores of New England, carrying illness along with goods they brought to trade for furs. In 1539, Hernando de Soto and his men landed in Florida and marched through much of the Southeast. Before de Soto reached interior settlements, messengers had spread newly introduced diseases, devastating Native populations. Later European arrivals found vastly different Native societies whose members were struggling to maintain and transmit what they had inherited.

In the wake of European colonization, most eastern Native people ceased making their own ceramics and instead began using brass kettles, other metal containers, or Euro-American china, although some managed to maintain their pottery-making traditions or, at the very least, the knowledge associated with them. Over the past several decades, individual Native artists and communities have worked to bring traditional ceramics back into practice, either by learning their ancestors' methods or by drawing on the past as an inspiration for works that utilize contemporary technology and materials. For all these artists, their work is a touchstone that binds them to the earth, to their pasts, and to their descendants, who will thank them for not forgetting and for not letting go.

"A tradition becomes a tradition by lasting. Some continue a tradition by using older ideas and bringing them into new work, and others continue a tradition by taking it further. There are very old pieces here and recent pieces. What's important to remember is that everything changed and is still changing. It changes, and we change."

—Peter B. Jones (Onondaga)

FELIPE SOLÍS

Mesoamerica The Cultural Wellspring
of Ancient Mexico and Central America

Thin orange ware is very
important to Teotihuacán
ceramics. Elegant and refined,
it was traded widely across
Mesoamerica. Among the most
prized examples of this style
were those painted by the
same methods used in creating ceremonial murals.

This figure represents
the ancient Aztec deity
Huehuetéotl, known as the
Old God, or god of fire, with
his wrinkled face and few
remaining teeth. Hunched over
with old age, he usually wears
on his head a brazier, a metal
container used to contain hot
coals. Because of his relationship to the hearth (and there-
fore the home), Huehuetéotl
was more of a household deity
than many other gods.

IN PRE-HISPANIC TIMES, a vast cultural territory we call Mesoamerica
extended from what is now central Mexico to Guatemala, Belize, Honduras, and
El Salvador. This area was home to some of the most advanced cultures the world
has ever known, and nowhere is this more evident than in its art, and specifically
its ceramics.

Archaeologists divide the history of Mesoamerica into the Pre-Classic, Classic,
and Post-Classic periods. Linguistic groups and particular artistic expressions
permit the division of the area into five regions as well: the Gulf Coast north and
south of present-day Veracruz; the central Mexican highlands; Oaxaca; the Maya
world of southern Mesoamerica; and western Mexico. I will recount a brief history of the area here, followed by a discussion of Mesoamerican ceramics.

Pre-Classic Period (2500 B.C.—A.D. 200)

Agriculture developed in Mexico around 2000 B.C., and with it came the first
sedentary settlements. Over the next thirty centuries, changes of great economic, political, and social complexity occurred, bringing with them a shift from
egalitarian societies to the emergence of city-states.

A number of important cultural practices were shared by different Pre-Classic
Mesoamerican peoples, including the use of the *coa* (a hoe-like tool used to plant
seeds); the cultivation of maize and the consumption of *nixtamal* (dried corn
cooked slowly in lime); the observance of time through the use of elaborate
calendars; and the creation of pyramids, ball-game courts, iron-ore mirrors, and
obsidian tools and ritual objects.

During this time, too, the first ceramics appeared in Mesoamerica and the
Olmec culture came to prominence. Near the end of the Pre-Classic period,
social stratification began.

Teotihuacán jar, A.D. 200–500. Toluca, Mexico. Modeled, appliquéd, and incised ceramic, 12.25 by 14 in. 16/6067

Classic Period (A.D. 200–900)

The Classic period brought the rise of numerous city-states, including important political and cultural centers such as Teotihuacán in the highlands and Monte Albán in present-day Oaxaca, and the consolidation of a vast area within Mesoamerica through a system of economic and social relationships. The region flourished, especially the arts and sciences, and the Maya, Zapotec, and Teotihuacán civilizations blossomed.

War became a major issue near the end of this era, as is reflected in the architecture of major cities such as Xochicalco, with its protective walls, and the battle mural paintings found at Cacaxtla. The emphasis on war in the region's political centers and the glorification of its rulers created the ideological basis for the Post-Classic period.

Post-Classic Period (A.D. 900–1521)

The Post-Classic period is marked by extensive migrations, strong militarism, intense commercial activity, and great cultural diversity. Artists fashioned wonderful creations in gold, silver, and copper. The early Post-Classic period is best represented by Tula, in central Mexico, and Chichen-Itza in the Maya lowlands, two of the greatest cities in Mesoamerica's long history. The late Post-Classic period witnessed the emergence of two powerful political entities: the Aztec empire and the Tarascan state of western Mexico. The era ended abruptly with the Spanish defeat of the Aztec Empire.

The Pottery of Mesoamerica

As might be expected of any art whose history spanned thousands of years, Mesoamerican ceramics vary widely in form, decoration, and even material. Clay deposits in Mesoamerica differ in quality and chemical composition by region and sometimes require great innovation from potters. The finest clays come from deposits along the Gulf Coast, and coarser ones from regions where limestone is found. Potters learned to add temper materials such as fine gravel or plant fibers to improve the quality and malleability of the clay. Open kilns were generally used for firing all types of clay, although the firing techniques used in the creation of plumbate vessels—known for their lustrous surfaces of orange and gray—remain a mystery, considering the closed atmosphere and high temperatures required to produce this ceramic effect.

The diverse indigenous groups of Mesoamerica used the same basic processes of manufacture: they modeled and molded the vessel, often in sections, before firing; polished it before and after applying a coat of slip; dried it in the shade; and fired it in an oxygen-starved (reductive) or oxygen-rich (oxidant) atmosphere.

The specific techniques used in the production and decoration of any given vessel allow us to appreciate that object within a cultural and chronological context. Some of the most important prefiring decorative techniques developed by Mesoamerican potters are polishing (also known as burnishing), painting,

During the late Classic period, a burial center for Maya nobility was established off the coast of what is now the Mexican state of Campeche. Known to us as Jaina, this island necropolis housed more than 20,000 tombs. Buried with the dead—and often positioned in their hands—were clay figures that represented individual people from across Maya society—priests and nobility, dancers and musicians, weavers and porters, the elderly and the infirm. Many Jaina and Jaina-style figures were actually musical instruments used in processional ceremonies and funerary rites.

There grew to be such a demand for these amazing, wonderfully realistic figures that artists shifted from building them by hand to using molds and other time-saving methods. For this reason, we find a considerable range in the quality of Jaina figures. The more highly detailed handbuilt figures are among the most spectacular works of Mesoamerican art, but they all offer us remarkable glimpses into Maya life.

Jaina-style Maya weaver, A.D. 400–800. Jaina Island, Campeche, Mexico. Modeled and appliquéd ceramic, 6 by 6.25 in. 23/2865

Jaina-style Maya drunkard, A.D. 400–800. Jaina Island, Campeche, Mexico. Modeled, appliquéd, and painted ceramic, 15 by 5.5 in. 23/2573

Pre-Classic stirrup-spout jar, 1100–800 B.C. Tlatilco, Mexico. Modeled and painted (prefiring) ceramic, 7.75 by 6.5 in. 22/9286

impressing, incising (very fine scratching), and excising and engraving (deeper scratching) the clay. Postfiring techniques include incision, excision, paint, fake cloisonné (in which incisions are filled with pigment), and the use of stucco (also known as the dry-fresco method). Before the arrival of European populations, Mesoamerican indigenous groups did not work with glaze; its use is characteristic of colonial and contemporary indigenous pottery.

Probably the best-known among Mesoamerican prefiring decorative techniques employs one or two tones of painting covering all or almost all the surface of the vessel, as seen in the example from Tlatilco (22/9286). A second method is section painting, featuring various geometric, naturalistic, or symbolic designs (23/7067). A third technique involves coating a section of a vessel with resins, which prohibit the impregnation of color and result in a negative-style decoration with various paint tonalities.

The Olmec and some cultures that preceded them used pointed instruments to make incisions in vessels before firing. The Olmec also popularized incision after a vessel had been fired. In this method, sections of the surface are scraped, then coated with mineral pigments, mainly cinnabar. Prefiring incision, perforation, and application of elements was a favorite technique of the Teotihuacán culture. In this way, the artists of Teotihuacán decorated the tripod vessels with straight walls that were used in commercial exchange outside the region (24/3383).

Remojadas male figure holding a bird, A.D. 300–600. Las Remojadas, Veracruz, Mexico. Modeled, appliquéd, and painted ceramic, 12.25 by 16 in. 23/6257

Teotihuacán cylindrical tripod jar with cover, A.D. 300–500. Teotihuacán, Mexico. Modeled, polished, carved, and appliquéd ceramic, 9 by 6.25 in. 24/3383

Teotihuacán cylindrical tripod jar, A.D. 300–500. Teotihuacán, Mexico. Modeled, stuccoed, and painted ceramic, 4.75 by 4.75 in. 22/9282

"Working with clay is a
driving force, a divine
force. All potters are
born of Mother Earth,
and we are not only
relatives, we are
brothers and sisters
in the clay. No matter
where some of these
pieces are from, we
can identify with their
common ideas of men
and women, birth, and
our humanity."

—Eleazar Navarrete Ramírez
(Nahua)

The most sophisticated expression of decoration in ancient Mexican ceramics is the so-called dry-fresco technique (22/9282). The vessel was covered with a thin stucco layer, and while this was still damp, pigment was applied, using a fixer that is unknown to us today. When the surface dried, it acquired an appearance similar to that of the indigenous murals of the region.

The Maya were the most advanced Mesoamerican artists in the application of paint over clay surfaces. In only one phase, before the first firing, they applied natural pigments as polychrome tonalities. Complex images and iconographic characters embody the resulting well-known style, found on plates and vases from the Classic period (24/4089).

During the Post-Classic period, potters in the central Mexican highlands and Oaxaca developed different polychrome decorative styles by copying the designs that appeared in the codices, or indigenous books. Unlike those made by the Maya, these vessels required a second firing at a lower temperature (23/6187).

Mesoamerican potters were masters who developed many ingenious techniques and produced works of incomparable beauty. Their efforts laid the foundation for the rich and varied ceramic traditions seen in Mexico and Central America today.

The location of the ancient pyramid Teocalli de Cholula and a later Toltec center, Cholula was at the time of Spanish arrival an Aztec city devoted to the worship of Quetzalcóatl, the plumed serpent wind god. In this extraordinary Cholula-Aztec piece (23/6187), Quetzalcóatl's symbolic headdress with long pendants is combined with the conical headdress of Xipe Tótec (god of spring and agriculture) and the red-and-black face painting typical of Tezcatlipoca. It's intriguing to see these three figures joined in the same work; Quetzalcóatl symbolizes civilization, light, and the forces of good, while Tezcatlipoca is the god of nighttime, war, evil, beauty, and destruction. Life, death, and rebirth are the work of Xipe Tótec, who flayed himself to give food to the people, just as the outer layer of the corn seed must separate if the seed is to germinate. Sometimes portrayed in gold, Xipe Tótec was worshiped through sacrifice. (Unusual in its portrayal of Xipe Tótec as a female entity, the Post-Classic figure from Colima [23/7831] wears the flayed skin of a sacrificial victim, the conical headdress, and the mask of human flesh characteristic of this god.)

The trinity-type Quetzalcóatl representation makes a pair with that of the corn and earth goddess (23/6188); both were found in the same cave. With her characteristic *chapopote* (tar) facial painting, Chicomecoatl represents the earth's fertility, and in one hand she carries *xicahuaztli,* sun rays.

Cholula-style Aztec male figure, A.D. 1350–1521. Puebla, Mexico. Modeled, painted (polychrome), and polished ceramic, 12 by 7 in. 23/6187

Cholula-style Aztec female figure, A.D. 1350–1521. Puebla, Mexico. Modeled, painted (polychrome), and polished ceramic, 13.5 by 7 in. 23/6188

Post-Classic West Mexico female figure with characteristics of the male Xipe Tótec (god of spring and agriculture), A.D. 1300–1521. Colima, Mexico. Modeled, appliquéd, and painted (postfiring) ceramic, 29 by 14 in. 23/7831

BRUCE BERNSTEIN

The Southwestern United States
Continuity and Change

OVER THE COURSE OF 2,000 YEARS, countless styles of pottery have emerged
and disappeared in the American Southwest. The ceramics we admire today reflect centuries of experimentation and adaptation to diverse and changing mar-
kets. Yet Pueblo potters also live within a culture whose deep foundation sustains
their work. A Pueblo person who lived a thousand years ago might marvel over or
lament new ceramic forms or designs, yet she or he would recognize the Pueblo
pottery of our time as Pueblo pottery. Many of the materials and techniques used
by potters, and the ideas they express in their work, have remained at the core of
Pueblo pottery. Among these constants is that clay is the very substance of life, the
same material from which the First People were made. Pueblo potters venerate
clay as a gift from Mother Earth. They speak to it, pray to it, revere it.

Gathering clay, too, is a prayerful activity. It is important to potters that they
are in a good frame of mind as they gather clay, and that they take only what they
need. When clay pits that have been used for generations become inaccessible
because of shifting streams, new road construction, or private non-Pueblo owner-
ship, people may stop manufacturing ceramics; alternatively, they may locate new
sources of clay. Where to find certain types of clays may be known to only a few,
and when they pass on, the knowledge of these locations may end, too. Potters
also trade for or buy some types of clay. Some potters are always looking for new
sources of clay, while others continue to use the same sources their family passed
on to them.

Once collected, the clay is dried, then soaked to remove impurities. Finally, it
is sieved to remove stones, roots, and other foreign matter. In the pueblos, potters' homes are easy to spot by the trash cans and other containers used to store or
soak clay outside their doors. Equal parts of a temper are added to purified clay to
reduce shrinkage and crackling during drying and firing. A variety of tempers have
been used; the most common are crushed rock, sand, and crushed potsherds.

Most potters work using the coil and scrape method. After the potter makes
the bottom of the pot, he or she places it in a base—sometimes known by its Tewa

Black-on-black plate, ca. 1930.
Made by Tonita Roybal (San
Ildefonso, 1892–1945) and Juan Cruz
Roybal (San Ildefonso, 1896–1990).
San Ildefonso Pueblo, New Mexico.
Modeled and painted ceramic,
1.5 by 11.5 in. 26/4234

name, *puki*. Fingers skillfully pinch together successive coils, or ropes, of clay to build up the walls of the pot. Coil junctures are smoothed with a curved-edge tool. Potters have adapted many implements for this purpose, including shaped gourds, Popsicle sticks, hairbrush handles, can lids, and kitchen knives. After the excess clay is scraped away to achieve a uniform thickness, the pot is smoothed. Most potters today use sandpaper to smooth their pottery; most consider it an improvement over the volcanic ash or tufa stones once used. The pots are then allowed to rest and dry.

Next the potter applies the slip, a watery clay mixture. While the layer of slip is still just slightly damp, the pot is polished with a smooth river stone. The slip must remain moist throughout the process, so even on a warm summer day, a potter will close up the house and pull the shades to help keep the humidity in the house. The most lustrous pieces can be coated with ten or even twenty coats of slip. Painted decoration is applied according to established traditions, but each potter will paint in his or her individual way. Potters have favorite places to work. Some work alone in a studio, preferring quiet to concentrate; others like to work at the kitchen table with family around. Some have their soap operas to watch while they work, or their favorite pottery-making music to listen to.

Firing is the test of a potter's work: any impurity or imperfection—for example, a small bubble of air in the clay—will show itself in the kiln by cracking the pottery, or worse, causing it to explode, damaging other pieces as well. Although some potters fire their work in electric kilns, most still fire outdoors. Potters usually fire in the early morning. If it has rained recently, the potter may light a fire to dry the ground before building the kiln. Increasingly, potters double-fire their pots—warming them in a preliminary fire, or the kitchen oven, and then firing them, to take some of the risk out of firing. For the main firing, kindling is stacked on the ground, and metal grates or other supports to keep the pots out of the fire are placed over the kindling. The fire is lighted and allowed to burn down. The pots are placed on the grate and more fuel—usually cow or sheep manure—is stacked around the pottery and ignited. Before the Spanish brought sheep and cows to the Southwest, only wood and bark were used to fire the kiln. Each fuel burns at a different rate and temperature. Most potters use manure that has been cut in blocks from corrals or collected as patties from fields. If a potter is making blackware, he or she smothers the fire with crushed dung, reducing the oxygen and carbonizing the pottery. The pots are removed from the fire while they are still warm, and the ashes are wiped off.

Some potters like to experiment, while others are conservative about firing, explaining, "It is the way we learned." Where metal grates, car parts, corrugated roofing, and other metal are used today to separate the pottery in a kiln and keep it out of the fire, large potsherds were once used. Many believe that it was Maria Martinez who first introduced metal into Pueblo pottery-firing through her use of cafeteria trays from the Los Alamos National Laboratory bordering San Ildefonso Pueblo. Other potters, particularly those at Acoma, perfected the use of coffee cans to shield individual pieces in the kiln and reduce

Plate, ca. 1957. Made by Maria Martinez (San Ildefonso, 1887–1980) and Popovi Da (San Ildefonso, 1921–1971). San Ildefonso Pueblo, New Mexico. Modeled and painted polychrome ceramic, 2.25 by 14.75 in. Indian Arts and Crafts Board Collection, Department of the Interior, at NMAI, 25/8830

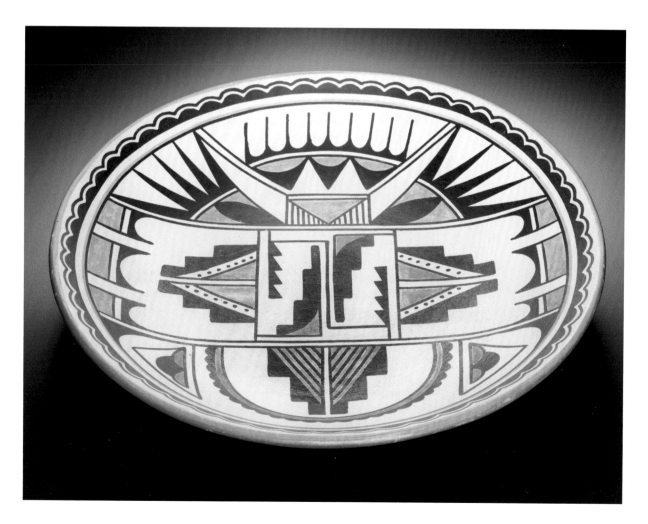

the chances of fire clouds developing during firing. Many potters today may live in Santa Fe or Albuquerque, yet they still bring their work back to the village to fire. One consistent innovation throughout the Pueblo world is that potters now fire a single piece, or maybe two or three pieces, at a time, whereas in the recent past many pots were fired at once.

Much of the iconography on Southwest pottery has remained conservative for centuries, for it mirrors the Pueblo world and is part of that world's whole. A pot and its design should be seen as existing within the landscape, rather than as a representation or embodiment of some aspect of it. To the potter's eye, the landscape begins before it reaches the pot's surface, and it continues across the surface and beyond. The designs on pottery also serve as prayers concerned with the bringing of moisture to the high desert of the pueblos. This is true not simply of rain-cloud motifs. There are mountains on pots because mountains are where clouds form. Feather designs represent birds, which are seen along the rivers during wet years, as well as individual feathers, prayers Pueblo people send to the clouds.

As the Spanish brought new crops into the Southwest during the seventeenth century, potters created new wares to prepare and serve new foods. Pueblo pottery helped integrate these foods into the Pueblo world. In the nineteenth century, as new groups of non-Natives arrived in the Southwest, Pueblo potters began to use iconography on their vessels to remind their people who they are. Some figurative pottery traditions still seen today trace their origins to some 130 years ago; now, as then, they serve to help integrate new people and events into Native culture. Antecedents of this practice can be traced back a thousand years.

Below left: Cochiti singing man, ca. 1890. Pueblo of Cochiti, New Mexico. Modeled and painted ceramic, 15.5 by 6.5 in. 6/6820

Below right: Standing clown figure, 2005. Made by Lisa Holt (Cochiti, b. 1980) and Harlan Reano (Santo Domingo, b. 1978). Albuquerque, New Mexico. Modeled and painted ceramic, 20.5 by 15 in. 26/5237

ENCOMPASSING FIGURES Pueblo ceramic figures often combine human forms with animal attributes, the familiar with the unfamiliar, in order to bring the unknown outside world into the safer confines of Pueblo society. Sometimes a figure is unmistakably a Pueblo man, recognizable by the depiction of his clothing or hair—or by the bag slung over his shoulder (19/6726). The men are usually standing with upraised eyes and hands, singing, their bodies covered with rich water symbolism. The Tesuque devil figure demonstrates the push and pull of Christianity in Pueblo people's lives. Interestingly, its posture is reminiscent of figures from pre-Columbian Mexico. Many early scholars speculated that Pueblo people were the ancestors of the vanquished Toltecs of central Mexico. Shrewd traders apparently seized on this notion, asking potters to duplicate pre-Columbian figurative pottery styles.

Academic research has shown that late-nineteenth-century Cochiti figures include traveling circus clowns. Their revival as a subject is part of a centuries-old tradition of Pueblo potters' finding inspiration in the past. Lisa Holt and Harlan Reano continue this tradition through their jaunty depiction (26/5237). Roxanne Swentzell's *Imprisoned Clown*—actually a Kossa, a being who might make fun of others to teach proper behavior—illustrates how stereotypes can imprison us. The figure is a reminder not to let our roles define us to the point that we are locked up in them.

Above left: Tesuque devil figure, ca. 1880. Tesuque Pueblo, New Mexico. Modeled and painted ceramic, 8.75 by 5 in. 7528

Below: Cochiti figurine, ca. 1880. Pueblo of Cochiti, New Mexico. Modeled and painted ceramic, 19 by 12.5 in. 19/6726

Above right: *Imprisoned Clown,* ca. 1999. Made by Roxanne Swentzell (Santa Clara, b. 1962). Santa Clara Pueblo, New Mexico. Modeled and painted ceramic, 18.25 by 17 in. 26/4272

"Potters can so easily lose the life of their work because they lose sight of that force inside them." —Jody Folwell (Santa Clara)

Pueblo culture is one continuous prayer for fertility—of rain, rivers, and clouds, as well as of the animal and plant worlds that water sustains. Making water pitchers using symbols of flowing water and rain; in the shapes of water fowl and snails or with designs of cranes and other water birds; and with the uplifted heads of men in song and prayer, Cochiti potters of the late nineteenth century created vessels that are prayers every time they are used. The flowers and vines winding around these pieces are expressions of fertility, as well, born of the rain and moisture brought through prayer.

All potters talk about clay's "living force." This life is the clay used to make pottery—the Earth itself—mixed with water, which is life in the high dry climate of the American Southwest. The earth holds water in lakes, rivers, ponds, and the like. Potters make vessels of earth to hold precious water, and use them to bring this life force into their homes.

Above: Tesuque double-spout pitcher, ca. 1890. Tesuque Pueblo, New Mexico. Modeled and painted Polychrome Two ceramic, 8.5 by 11.25 in. 6/201

Below: Cochiti duckling figure, ca. 1880. Pueblo of Cochiti, New Mexico. Modeled and painted ceramic, 6 by 8.5 in. 11/5015

Above: Cochiti singing-man pitcher, ca. 1890. Pueblo of Cochiti, New Mexico. Modeled and painted ceramic, 9 by 8.75 in. 7502

Right: Cochiti animal-human figurine, ca. 1890. Pueblo of Cochiti, New Mexico. Modeled and painted ceramic, 10.75 by 7.75 in. 21/1134

Until the late 1800s pottery was a fundamental part of daily Pueblo life, and the majority of pottery was made for household use. Pottery water coolers, storage containers, and pots, bowls, and dishes to prepare and serve food were staples of Pueblo homes and the homes of Hispanic settlers. By the mid-to-late 1880s, however, factory-made metalware and ceramics were replacing handmade pottery.

In the late 1800s, the sale of pottery to collectors became a source of income for Pueblo families. It is a sad truth that American interest in Indian art increased as European-American society forced changes upon Indian people. The suppression of Native religions began with Contact and continued in the 1870s and '80s under U.S. government "civilization regulations" that remained in force for sixty years. Under these regulations, Indian children were sent to boarding schools where they could be punished for speaking their own language or showing any other outward sign that they were thinking of home. The Pueblo peoples' survival was further assaulted as water rights were systematically and illegally taken from their villages.

During these years of loss and repression, the pueblos were, in many ways, increasingly closed to the outside world. Out of sight of Anglo authorities, Pueblo communities became adamantly protective of their beliefs and practices. Pottery served as a primary means for Pueblo people to convey to themselves and to the outside world their identity, origins, and consciousness. At the same time, Pueblo potters began to create new styles of pottery to appeal to the non-Pueblo market. Some of these changes build upon traditional styles and designs; others are wholly new.

Pueblo pottery-making has survived because Pueblo people continue to find meaning in it. One way to understand the continuum of Pueblo pottery is to view art as having internal and external features. External features evolve in response to the ever-changing world around us. Inner features—intensely held values and understandings—continue to tell Pueblo people who they are and help them make sense of the world. Within the Pueblo worldview, Creation is ongoing, not something that happened long ago in another place. Native art, too, is about a state of becoming, as well as a state of being: the act of making of an object is as important as the finished piece.

In the non-Native marketplace, pottery is sometimes characterized as craft, rather than creative art, and it is assumed that potters follow an established norm seen as "Pueblo pottery." Certainly there are potters who execute time-honored traditions in shape, design, and materials. Yet innovators, too, are deeply rooted in the same pottery traditions. Decorative and technical excellence, even when expressed in new ways by individual potters, is important to the community's collective sense of itself and its place in the long history of Pueblo culture. The act of making pottery tends to keep people in the villages and within a Pueblo worldview.

It is quite possible that there are more Pueblo potters working in the Southwest today than at any other time in history. Throughout the Americas, contemporary Native individuals and societies are using the arts to proclaim their determination to survive. Between the Native and non-Native worlds, art remains a negotiated space, where Native people can tell their own stories, in their own ways, and where others are welcome to listen. Although some people may lament the changes in designs, tools, materials, and forms that take place whenever different cultures meet, we have only to look to the Pueblo world to understand how new ideas keep traditions vital. Pueblo potters, like artists everywhere, add the experiences and ideas of their time to the vast reservoir of their people's cultural history. In this way, whether made for home use or for sale, with indigenous or introduced materials, pottery endures as an integral part of the Pueblo world.

Osama Ken-Barbie, 2004. Made by Susan Folwell (Santa Clara, b. 1970) and Franzie Weldgen (b. 1972). Tucson, Arizona. Modeled and painted ceramic, 5.5 by 19.5 in. 26/4621

NARRATIVES "In the world I come from, the tradition is long and is remembered very well and the history of our world will continue on for a very long time to come." —Jody Folwell (Santa Clara)

Each and every pot is a narrative, a story, whether autobiographical, evoking the landscape, or synthesizing new ideas. And the technology of pottery-making is as much narrative as the shapes and designs on finished vessels. Within Pueblo culture clay simultaneously mirrors life, is symbol of that life, and is a living being. Jody Folwell puts this very well: "Clay is our life, clay tells us the stories of where we have been, who we are, and where we are going. Its voice is loud and clear, declaring, 'We are still here.'"

We recognize the narrative references of Susan Folwell's *Osama Ken-Barbie* bowl because we have lived this history together. Other pottery is more personal. Our appreciation of Diego Romero's two classically depicted men playing lacrosse is heightened by learning that he is honoring the lacrosse traditions of his new wife and family. His use of neo-Grecian males is intended to remind us that Pueblo culture has deep classical roots, too. Other ideas may be lost to time: Why are cranes carrying bird nets which seem to contain humans? An antelope appears comprehensible until we notice its body is made of a blanket, and it has badger paws and human feet.

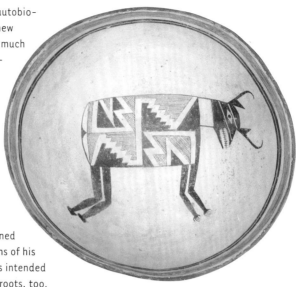

Above: Mimbres bowl,
A.D. 1000–1150. Grant County, New Mexico. Modeled and painted ceramic, 5.5 by 11.75 in. 24/3196

Left: *Stickball,* 2004. Made by Diego Romero (Cochiti, b. 1964). Oklahoma. Modeled and painted ceramic, 6.25 by 12.25 in. 26/5249

Right: Ancestral Pueblo bowl,
A.D. 875–1000. Pueblo Bonito, Chaco Canyon, New Mexico. Modeled and painted Red Mesa grayware ceramic, 4.5 by 9.5 in. 5/3048

Ceramics from NMAI's Collections

Valdivia female figurine,
3000–1500 B.C. Valdivia,
Province of Guayas, Ecuador.
Modeled ceramic, 5.25 by
1.75 in. 24/8726

**Cupisnique stirrup-spout
bottle with mouse figure,**
600–300 B.C. Chongoyape, Department of Lambayeque, Peru.
Modeled and stamped ceramic,
8.5 by 6 in. 16/1971

**Cupisnique stirrup-spout
bottle in the form of a woman washing her hair,** 600–100
B.C. Tembladera, Department of
Cajamarca, Peru. Modeled and
punctated ceramic, 9 by 6 in.
24/6875

**Cupisnique bridge-handle
bottle with parrot figure,**
500–100 B.C. Tembladera,
Department of Cajamarca, Peru.
Modeled and incised ceramic,
10 by 11.5 in. 24/3538

**Cupisnique snake-shaped,
stirrup-spout bottle,** 500–100
B.C. Tembladera, Department of
Cajamarca, Peru. Modeled and
incised ceramic, 8 by 6.75 in.
24/3535

**Cupisnique musician playing
panpipes,** 400 B.C.–A.D. 100.
Tembladera, Department of Cajamarca, Peru. Modeled, punctated, and appliquéd ceramic,
6.75 by 3.75 in. 24/1885

**Chorrera bowl depicting a
dead man,** 600 B.C.–A.D. 1.
Puerto Callo, Joa, Province of
Manabí, Ecuador. Modeled,
stamped, and painted ceramic,
6.75 by 6.5 in. 24/4326

24/8726

16/1971

24/6875

24/3538

24/3535

24/1885

24/4326

Paracas feline-shaped, bridge-handle bottle, 400–200 B.C. Cahuachi, Department of Ica, Peru. Modeled, incised, and painted ceramic, 6 by 9 in. 23/8375

Paracas bowl with hunter and feline designs, 400–100 B.C. Paracas, Department of Ica, Peru. Incised and painted (postfiring) ceramic, 3.75 by 6.75 in. 22/8787

Nazca double-spout-and-bridge bottle depicting chile peppers, A.D. 100–500. Nazca Valley, Department of Ica, Peru. Modeled and painted ceramic, 8.5 by 7.25 in. 11/2810

Nazca stirrup-spout bottle in the form of a burden bearer, A.D. 100–600. Nazca Valley, Department of Ica, Peru. Molded and painted ceramic, 9.75 by 6 in. 11/2597

Nazca canteen depicting water and fish, A.D. 100–600. Nazca Valley, Department of Ica, Peru. Modeled and painted ceramic, 8 by 7.5 in. 11/2807

Nazca trumpet, A.D. 200–500. Department of Cusco, Peru. Modeled and painted ceramic, 3.25 by 12.5 in. 15/9414

23/8375

22/8787

11/2810

11/2597

11/2807

15/9414

ANDES

Nazca drum, A.D. 200–500. Nazca Valley, Department of Ica, Peru. Modeled and painted ceramic, 16 by 8.75 in. 21/9024

Nazca cup depicting warriors dancing, A.D. 300–600. Nazca Valley, Department of Ica, Peru. Modeled and painted ceramic, 6.75 by 4.5 in. 11/2516

Nazca cylindrical cup depicting trophy heads and a winged being, A.D. 300–600. Nazca Valley, Department of Ica, Peru. Modeled and painted ceramic, 5.5 by 2.75 in. 11/2503

Nazca cylindrical cup depicting fish and centipedes, A.D. 300–600. Nazca Valley, Department of Ica, Peru. Modeled and painted ceramic, 5.25 by 2 in. 11/2507

Nazca spiral-ridge cup depicting winged beings, A.D. 300–600. Nazca Valley, Department of Ica, Peru. Modeled and painted ceramic, 8.25 by 7.75 in. 11/2763

Nazca globular pot depicting condors and penguins, A.D. 300–600. Nazca Valley, Department of Ica, Peru. Modeled and painted ceramic, 7.75 by 9.25 in. 11/2891

Nazca double-spout-and-bridge bottle, A.D. 300–600. Nazca Valley, Department of Ica, Peru. Modeled and painted ceramic, 8 by 8 in. 11/2781

21/9024

11/2516

11/2503

11/2763

11/2507

11/2891

11/2781

Nazca double-spout-and-bridge bottle in the form of a snake, A.D. 300–600. Nazca Valley, Department of Ica, Peru. Modeled and painted ceramic, 4 by 7.25 in. 11/2566

Nazca globular jar, A.D. 700–900. Nazca Valley, Department of Ica, Peru. Modeled and painted ceramic, 7.25 by 7.25 in. 11/2798

Moche toad-shaped, stirrup-spout bottle, A.D. 1–200. Northern coast of Peru. Modeled and painted ceramic, 6.5 by 7.5 in. 23/6189

Moche stirrup-spout bottle in the form of a squatting man, A.D. 1–400. Trujillo, Department of La Libertad, Peru. Modeled and painted ceramic, 6.25 by 6 in. 5/1890

Moche stirrup-spout bottle in the form of a trophy head, A.D. 100–400. Tembladera, Department of Cajamarca, Peru. Molded, incised, and painted ceramic, 12.25 by 6.5 in. 24/7645

11/2566

11/2798

23/6189

24/7645

5/1890

Moche stirrup-spout bottle in the form of a seated nobleman, A.D. 100–300. Moche, Department of La Libertad, Peru. Molded and painted ceramic, 6.5 by 7.5 in. 24/7955

Moche stirrup-spout bottle depicting a healing scene, A.D. 200–400. Northern coast of Peru. Modeled and painted ceramic, 7.5 by 6.5 in. 7433

Moche portrait cup, A.D. 300–600. Northern coast of Peru. Molded, painted, and incised ceramic, 6 by 6.5 in. 9/7245

Moche whistle in the form of a pacay or huava fruit *(Inga feuillei),* A.D. 400–600. Trujillo, Department of La Libertad, Peru. Molded ceramic, 12.5 by 3 in. 12/9889

Moche whistle in the form of a tillandsia plant (Spanish moss), A.D. 400–600. Northern coast of Peru. Molded ceramic, 10.5 by 6 in. 19/9297

Moche jar in the form of a musician playing a drum, A.D. 500–900. Northern coast of Peru. Modeled and painted ceramic, 9.75 by 7 in. 22/3546

24/7955

7433

9/7245

12/9889

22/3546

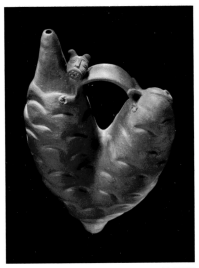

19/9297

Moche globular bottle with ritual representations, A.D. 800–1100. Santa Province, Department of Ancash, Peru. Modeled and painted ceramic, 6.5 by 5.75 in. 24/3816

Recuay pitcher with feline figure, A.D. 100–500. Peru. Modeled and painted ceramic, 7.25 by 6 in. 23/7006

Vicus stirrup-spout bottle, A.D. 200–500. Ayabaca, Department of Piura, Peru. Modeled and painted ceramic, 10 by 6 in. 23/8938

La Tolita drum with three faces, A.D. 100–500. La Tolita, Province of Esmeraldas, Ecuador. Modeled and painted ceramic, 22 by 12 in. 24/6659

Guangala whistle, A.D. 100–900. Guangala, Province of Manabí, Ecuador. Modeled and incised ceramic, 9.25 by 3.5 in. 24/6607

Bahía figure of a cross-legged man, A.D. 100–900. Los Esteros, Province of Manabí, Ecuador. Modeled and painted ceramic, 20 by 10 in. 24/462

24/3816

23/7006

23/8938

24/6659

24/462

24/6607

Bahía musician playing panpipes, A.D. 100–900. Cerro Jaboncillo, Province of Manabí, Ecuador. Modeled and incised ceramic, 6 by 4 in. 1/6004

Bahía healer or priest, A.D. 100–900. Cerro Jaboncillo, Province of Manabí, Ecuador. Modeled ceramic, 10.5 by 6 in. 1/6272

Bahía female figurine, A.D. 100–900. Los Esteros, Province of Manabí, Ecuador. Modeled and painted ceramic, 5.25 by 2.25 in. 23/9930

Bahía double-lobed whistling bottle with shaman figurine, A.D. 100–900. Jipijapa, Bahía, Ecuador. Modeled and painted ceramic, 8.75 by 13.75 in. 24/3220

Jama-Coaque male-figure whistle, A.D. 400–1500. Jama-Coaque, Ecuador. Modeled and painted ceramic, 6.25 by 4.5 in. 24/4823

Tiwanaku pedestal-based censer with condor, A.D. 600–900. Tiwanaku, Department of La Paz, Bolivia. Molded and painted ceramic, 10.5 by 13.5 in. 24/4450

Tiwanaku pedestal-based censer with jaguar, A.D. 600–900. Tiwanaku, Department of La Paz, Bolivia. Modeled and painted ceramic, 11.25 by 12 in. 20/6313

1/6004

1/6272

23/9930

24/3220

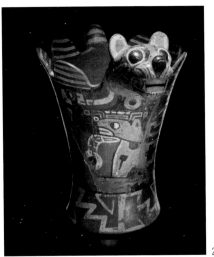

24/4823

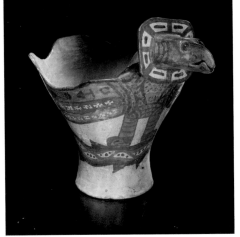

24/4450

20/6313

ANDES

Tiwanaku bottle depicting Wiraqocha (the staff god), A.D. 700–1300. Peru. Modeled and painted ceramic, 7.25 by 5 in. 23/6464

Tiwanaku bottle depicting a llama or alpaca, A.D. 1000–1200. Tiwanaku, Department of La Paz, Bolivia. Modeled and painted ceramic, 8 by 9.25 in. 20/6317

Wari double-spout-and-bridge bottle depicting condors, A.D. 800–1000. Doña María, central coast of Peru. Modeled and painted ceramic, 5.5 by 7.75 in. 24/3817

Wari bottle, A.D. 800–1000. Chocay, Department of Lima, Peru. Modeled and painted ceramic, 7.73 by 10.25 in. 23/1070

Panzaleo canteen in the form of a pregnant woman, A.D. 900–1500. Ecuador. Modeled and painted ceramic, 12 by 7.5 in. 24/6655

Tuza triple-body vessel with basket handle, A.D. 1000–1500. El Angel, Province of Carchi, Ecuador. Modeled and painted ceramic, 5.25 by 7 in. 3/360

Tuza-Piartal whistle in the form of a land snail, A.D. 1100–1500. Huaca, Province of Carchi, Ecuador. Modeled and painted ceramic, 3 by 5.5 in. 3/875

23/6464

20/6317

24/3817

23/1070

24/6655

3/360

3/875

ANDES

Piartal footed plate depicting dancers, A.D. 1100–1500. Province of Carchi, Ecuador. Modeled and painted ceramic, 3.25 by 7 in. 23/7003

Capuli footed plate, A.D. 1100–1600. El Angel, Province of Carchi, Ecuador. Modeled and painted ceramic, 3.5 by 8.25 in. 3/324

Lambayeque bridge-handle whistling bottle depicting maize deity, A.D. 1100–1600. Chicama Valley, Department of La Libertad, Peru. Molded ceramic, 9 by 7.75 in. 11/1359

Chimú stirrup-spout bottle in the form of a duck, A.D. 1100–1400. Northern coast of Peru. Molded and modeled ceramic, 9.5 by 9.5 in. 23/6883

Chimú bottle in the form of a *loshi* (squash), A.D. 1200–1400. Northern coast of Peru. Modeled ceramic, 11.25 by 6.5 in. 15/1457

23/7003

3/324

11/1359

23/6883

15/1457

Casma bottle in the form of *pepinos* or *kachum* (melon pears), A.D. 1200–1400. Central coast of Peru. Modeled and painted ceramic, 6 by 8 in. 19/9298

Chuquibamba pitcher depicting llamas, A.D. 1100–1600. Arequipa, Department of Arequipa, Peru. Modeled and painted ceramic, 5.75 by 5.25 in. 14/5496

Inka double-chambered bottle with man and llama figures, ca. A.D. 1500. Chan Chan site, Trujillo, Department of La Libertad, Peru. Modeled ceramic, 6.5 by 9.25 in. 14/3673

Inka vessel depicting a man carrying an *arybalo* (jar), A.D. 1500–1600. Northern coast of Peru. Modeled and painted ceramic, 9.75 by 5.5 in. 20/6477

Inka *paqcha* (ritual vessel) depicting a llama head with *arybalo* (jar) on top, A.D. 1500–1600. Department of Cusco, Peru. Modeled and painted ceramic, 8 by 9 in. 16/4835

Inka *qocha* (ritual vessel), A.D. 1500–1600. Tiwanaku, Department of La Paz, Bolivia. Modeled and painted ceramic, 1.5 by 6.25 in. 20/6341

Inka miniature vessel, A.D. 1500–1600. Tiwanaku, Department of La Paz, Bolivia. Modeled and painted ceramic, 3.75 by 4.5 in. 20/6347

19/9298

14/5496

14/3673

16/4835

20/6477

20/6347

20/6341

ANDES

Chancay jar, A.D. 1100–1500. Chimbote, Department of Ancash, Peru. Modeled and painted ceramic, 17.25 by 8.5 in. 16/1060

Chimborazo pedestal plate, 1880–1920. Chambo, Province of Chimborazo, Ecuador. Modeled and glazed ceramic, 9 by 9.5 in. 1/1596

Aymara ring-shaped *paqcha* (ritual vessel) with animal heads, 1880–1940. La Paz, Department of La Paz, Bolivia. Modeled ceramic, 3.25 by 7.5 in. 6/3307

Quechua medicinal or ceremonial cup, 1930–1950. Department of Cochabamba, Bolivia. Modeled and painted ceramic, 4 by 4.5 in. 20/6386

Quechua vessel depicting a man carrying an *arybalo* (jar), 2005. Raqchi, Department of Cusco, Peru. Modeled and painted ceramic, 9 by 4.25 in. 26/5355

Quechua two-headed llama, 2005. Raqchi, Department of Cusco, Peru. Modeled ceramic, 6.5 by 6.5 in. 26/5356

1/1596

16/1060

6/3307

20/6386

26/5355

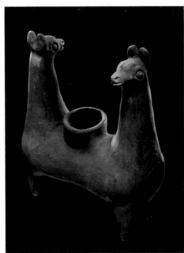

26/5356

Quechua jar, 2005. Raqchi, Department of Cusco, Peru. Modeled and painted ceramic, 12 by 7.5 in. 26/5351

Lidded bowl with puma handles, 2005. Made by Exaltación Mamani Amaro (Quechua, b. 1962) and Irma Rodríguez Moroco (Quechua, b. 1969). Raqchi, Department of Cusco, Peru. Modeled and painted ceramic, 2 by 3.5 in. 26/5291

Qero (ritual vessel), 2005. Made by Exaltación Mamani Amaro (Quechua, b. 1962) and Irma Rodríguez Moroco (Quechua, b. 1969). Raqchi, Department of Cusco, Peru. Modeled and painted ceramic, 2.5 by 3.25 in. 26/5293

Fruit plate, 2005. Made by Exaltación Mamani Amaro (Quechua, b. 1962) and Irma Rodríguez Moroco (Quechua, b. 1969). Raqchi, Department of Cusco, Peru. Modeled and painted ceramic, 3 by 2.25 in. 26/5272

Lidded bowls, 2005. Made by Exaltación Mamani Amaro (Quechua, b. 1962) and Irma Rodríguez Moroco (Quechua, b. 1962). Raqchi, Department of Cusco, Peru. Modeled and painted ceramic, 1 by 1.25 in. and 1.25 by 1.5 in. 26/5289

26/5351

26/5291

26/5293

26/5272

26/5289

THE DEPTFORD CULTURE

Middle Woodland (Deptford culture) jar, 100 B.C.–A.D. 100. Hall Mound, Wakulla County, Florida. Modeled, incised, and painted ceramic, 8.75 by 4.5 in. 17/3982

Middle Woodland (Deptford culture) vessel in the form of a West Indian marine worm shell, 100 B.C.–A.D. 100. Pierce Mounds, Franklin County, Florida. Modeled and painted ceramic, 6.75 by 8 in. 17/4993

DUCKS AND PRIESTS

Late Mississippian bowl depicting a wood duck, A.D. 1300–1500. Stewart County, Tennessee. Modeled ceramic, 5.25 by 9.5 in. 8/2537

Late Mississippian bowl depicting a mythical bird, A.D. 1350–1550. Sawyers Landing, Arkansas County, Arkansas. Modeled and incised ceramic, 6.5 by 10.25 in. 17/4167

MOUNDVILLE

Late Mississippian bottle with moth antenna design, A.D. 1300–1500. Moundville site, Hale County, Alabama. Modeled and painted ceramic, 8 by 6.25 in. 17/1432

Late Mississippian bottle with falcon design, A.D. 1300–1550. Moundville site, Hale County, Alabama. Modeled and engraved ceramic, 4 by 5 in. 17/1424

Late Mississippian bottle with raised hand and arm bones, A.D. 1350–1500. Hickman County, Kentucky. Modeled and appliquéd ceramic, 7.5 by 8 in. 4/8063

17/3982

17/4993

8/2537

17/4167

17/1432

4/8063

17/1424

Late Mississippian Underwater Panther–Great Serpent bowl, A.D. 1300–1550. Rhodes Place, Crittenden County, Arkansas. Modeled and incised ceramic, 7.75 by 9.5 in. 17/4147

Late Mississippian pot with flared rim representing a serpent's mouth, A.D. 1300–1600. Williams Island, Hamilton County, Tennessee. Modeled and appliquéd ceramic, 6.5 by 9.75 in. 19/8059

Late Mississippian vessel in the form of the Underwater Panther, A.D. 1400–1600. Rose Mound, Cross County, Arkansas. Modeled and painted ceramic, 9.75 by 9.75 in. 17/3425

Caddoan bottle with serpent design, A.D. 1500–1700. Arkansas. Modeled and engraved ceramic, 6.25 by 6.25 in. 21/5859

WOODPECKERS
AND WARRIORS

Late Mississippian bottle with woodpecker design, A.D. 1300–1550. Moundville site, Hale County, Alabama. Modeled and engraved ceramic, 7 by 8 in. 17/3363

Late Mississippian bowl in the form of a warrior wearing a crest, A.D. 1400–1600. Nashville, Davidson County, Tennessee. Modeled ceramic, 5 by 9.5 in. 4/8296

17/4147

19/8059

17/3425

21/5859

17/3363

4/8296

Caddoan bottle, A.D. 1500–1700. Keno Place, Morehouse Parish, Louisiana. Modeled and incised ceramic, 7.5 by 7.25 in. 17/1444

Caddoan bottle, A.D. 1500–1700. Glendora Place, Ouachita Parish, Louisiana. Modeled and engraved ceramic, 6.5 by 7 in. 17/3711

Caddoan bottle, A.D. 1500–1700. Glendora Place, Ouachita Parish, Louisiana. Modeled and engraved ceramic, 4.75 by 5.25 in. 17/3726

Caddoan squared bottle, A.D. 1500–1700. Foster Place, Lafayette County, Arkansas. Modeled and engraved ceramic with red pigment, 6.25 by 5.25 in. 17/4701

Intertwining Scrolls, 2005. Made by Jereldine Redcorn (Caddo/Potawatomi, b. 1939). Norman, Oklahoma. Modeled and engraved ceramic with red pigment, 8 by 6.7 in. 26/5160

17/1444

17/3711

17/3726

17/4701

26/5160

Late Mississippian pot with strap handles, A.D. 1300–1600. Rhodes Place, Crittenden County, Arkansas. Modeled, incised, and punctated ceramic, 9 by 10 in. 17/3656

St. Lawrence Iroquoian castellated cooking pot, A.D. 1500–1600. Jefferson County, New York. Modeled and incised ceramic, 8 by 8.5 in. 9/3208

Late Woodland castellated pot, A.D. 1500–1700. Brookfield, Fairfield County, Connecticut. Modeled and incised ceramic, 9 by 8 in. 11/2946

EFFIGY PIPES

St. Lawrence Iroquoian pipe with three faces, A.D. 1400–1500. Jefferson County, New York. Modeled and incised ceramic, 2.25 by 4.75 in. 24/2427

Neutral or Wenro pipe, A.D. 1620–1650. Lake Medad, Ontario, Canada. Modeled and incised ceramic, 4 by 4.75 in. 5/4876

17/3656

9/3208

11/2946

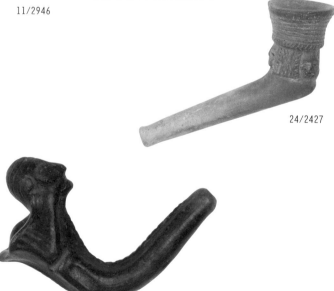

24/2427

5/4876

Caddoan bottle with three-lobed base, A.D. 1200–1500. Le Flore County, Oklahoma. Modeled ceramic, 9 by 8 in. 20/742

Caddoan tripod bottle, A.D. 1200–1550. Yell County, Arkansas. Modeled and incised ceramic, 11 by 9.5 in. 19/7979

Late Mississippian bottle (also known as "The Triune Vessel") in the form of three heads, A.D. 1350–1550. Chestnut Mound, Smith County, Tennessee. Modeled and appliquéd ceramic, 7 by 8 in. 23/6734

WEATHER, WIND, AND WATER

Late Mississippian (Fort Walton culture) bowl with frog design, A.D. 1350–1500. Choctawhatchee Bay, Point Washington, Walton County, Florida. Modeled and incised ceramic, 7.75 by 16 in. 17/3821

Late Mississippian (Fort Walton culture) gourd-shaped bowl, A.D. 1350–1500. Gulf County, Florida. Modeled and incised ceramic, 3.5 by 7 in. 17/4045

Late Mississippian frog-shaped jar, A.D. 1400–1500. Big Bone Bank site, Posey County, Indiana. Modeled ceramic, 3.75 by 7 in. 5/5655

20/742

19/7979

23/6734

17/3821

17/4045

5/5655

Late Mississippian bottle with ogee design, A.D. 1350–1450. Big Bone Bank site, Posey County, Indiana. Modeled and appliquéd ceramic, 6.5 by 9.5 in. 5/5721

Late Mississippian bowl depicting a lightning whelk shell (*Busycon sinistrum*), A.D. 1350–1450. Big Bone Bank site, Posey County, Indiana. Modeled and painted ceramic, 5 by 13.75 in. 5/5931

Late Mississippian bottle with two faces, A.D. 1350–1450. Big Bone Bank site, Posey County, Indiana. Modeled and painted ceramic, 7 by 5.25 in. 5/5990

Late Mississippian bowl, A.D. 1350–1450. Big Bone Bank site, Posey County, Indiana. Modeled ceramic, 6.75 by 9.25 in. 5/6225

CLARENCE
BLOOMFIELD MOORE

Late Woodland (Weeden Island culture) squared jar, A.D. 200–700. Hare Hammock, Bay County, Florida. Modeled, incised, punctated, and painted ceramic, 8.5 by 5 in. 17/4033

Late Woodland (Weeden Island culture) jar with rolled rim, A.D. 200–700. Choctawhatchee Bay, Point Washington, Walton County, Florida. Modeled and incised ceramic, 3.25 by 6.25 in. 17/4517

5/5721

5/5990

5/5931

5/6225

17/4517

17/4033

Late Woodland (Weeden Island culture) footed jar, A.D. 250–500. Hare's Landing, Decatur County, Georgia. Modeled, incised, and punctated ceramic with red pigment, 7.75 by 4.75 in. 17/4454

Late Woodland (Weeden Island culture) footed bowl with owl head, A.D. 250–800. Mound west of Burnt Mill Creek, Bay County, Florida. Modeled and incised ceramic, 5 by 10.25 in. 8/4157

Late Woodland (Weeden Island culture) jar with scalloped rim, A.D. 250–800. Crystal River, Citrus County, Florida. Modeled, incised, and punctated ceramic, 4.75 by 6.5 in. 17/3870

Caddoan squared bottle, A.D. 1000–1300. Mound Landing, Morehouse Parish, Louisiana. Modeled and incised ceramic, 8.5 by 6 in. 17/1441

Caddoan castellated jar with strap handles, A.D. 1200–1500. Haley Place, Miller County, Arkansas. Modeled, incised, appliquéd, and punctated ceramic, 8.5 by 4.75 in. 17/4639

17/4454

8/4157

17/3870

17/1441

17/4639

Caddoan bottle, A.D. 1500–1700. Glendora Place, Ouachita Parish, Louisiana. Modeled and engraved ceramic, 8.5 by 8.5 in. 17/3715

Late Mississippian bottle, A.D. 1400–1550. Miller Place, Poinsett County, Arkansas. Modeled and painted ceramic, 10.25 by 7.25 in. 17/1398

Late Mississippian bottle in the form of a woman giving birth, A.D. 1400–1600. Bradley Place, Crittenden County, Arkansas. Modeled and appliquéd ceramic, 7.5 by 6.5 in. 17/4161

Late Mississippian bottle, A.D. 1400–1600. Douglas, Lincoln County, Arkansas. Modeled and slipped ceramic, 8.25 by 8 in. 17/3317

Late Mississippian globular bottle, A.D. 1450–1600. Rose Place, Cross County, Arkansas. Modeled and incised ceramic, 8.5 by 8.75 in. 17/4224

Guale jar, A.D. 1600–1650. Creighton Island, McIntosh County, Georgia. Modeled and stamped ceramic, 22.5 by 18 in. 17/4489

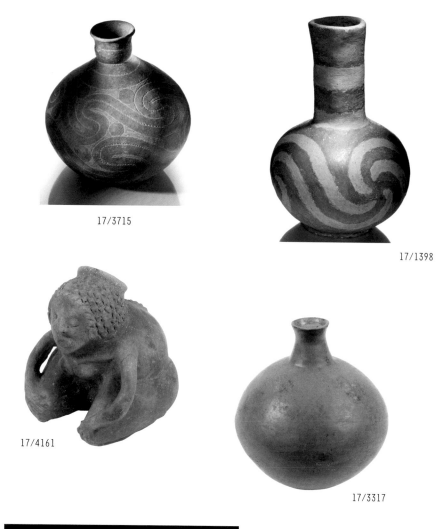

17/3715

17/1398

17/4161

17/3317

17/4224

17/4489

EASTERN

Late Mississippian bottle,
A.D. 1400–1600. Carden Bottom site, Yell County, Arkansas. Modeled, incised, and appliquéd ceramic, 8.25 by 8 in. 12/6549

Late Mississippian jar,
A.D. 1350–1550. Blytheville, Mississippi County, Arkansas. Modeled, incised, and painted ceramic, 6.25 by 8 in. 5/2981

Late Mississippian bottle,
A.D. 1300–1500. Monette, Craighead County, Arkansas. Modeled and painted ceramic, 7 by 7 in. 5/1082

Late Mississippian bottle in the form of a human leg trophy with protruding femur, A.D. 1400–1600. Franklin, Williamson County, Tennessee. Modeled ceramic, 8.5 by 4.75 in. 7387

CADDOAN VESSELS

Caddoan jar with flared rim,
A.D. 1100–1300. Washington, Hempstead County, Arkansas. Modeled, incised, and punctated ceramic, 6 by 3.75 in. 5/6281

Caddoan spherical seed jar,
A.D. 1400–1600. Hot Springs County, Arkansas. Modeled ceramic, 9.5 by 10.5 in. 6641

12/6549

5/2981

7387

5/1082

5/6281

6641

Late Woodland corncob-shaped jar, A.D. 1200–1700. Fairfield County, Connecticut. Modeled and cord-wrapped-stick-impressed ceramic, 1.75 x 3.25 in. 5/3482

Susquehannock jar, A.D. 1645–1665. Columbia, Lancaster County, Pennsylvania. Molded and cord-impressed ceramic, 6.75 by 6.25 in. 22/446

CONTEMPORARY WORKS

Jar, 1973. Made by Sara Ayers (Catawba, 1919–2002). South Carolina. Modeled and polished ceramic, 7.25 by 11 in. 24/8995

Spider vase, 1986. Made by Lucy Dean Reed (Cherokee, b. 1957). North Carolina. Modeled and incised stoneware, 6.25 by 4.75 in. Indian Arts and Crafts Board Collection, Department of the Interior, at the National Museum of the American Indian. 26/1111

9-11, 2001. Made by Peter B. Jones (Onondaga, b. 1947). Versailles, New York. Wheel-thrown and modeled stoneware, 11 by 9 in. 26/5179

Caddoan Head Pot, 2005. Made by Jereldine Redcorn (Caddo/Potawatomi, b. 1939). Norman, Oklahoma. Modeled and engraved ceramic with red pigment, 8.75 by 8.25 in. 26/5161

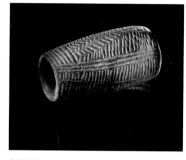

5/3482

22/446

24/8995

26/1111

26/5161

26/5179

Olmec male figure,
1500–800 B.C. Puebla, Mexico.
Modeled, painted (cinnabar),
and polished ceramic, 2 by
1.5 in. 23/3131

**Olmec ritual bottle depicting
mythological birds,**
1100–800 B.C. Las Bocas,
Puebla, Mexico. Modeled,
painted (postfiring), polished,
and incised ceramic, 8.25 by
6 in. 24/1148

Olmec bowl, 1100–800 B.C.
Tlapacoya, Mexico, Mexico.
Modeled, polished, and incised
ceramic, 2.25 by 11.25 in.
23/4953

**Pre-Classic stirrup-spout
jar,** 1100–800 B.C. Tlatilco,
Mexico, Mexico. Modeled and
painted (prefiring) ceramic,
7.75 by 6.5 in. 22/9286

Pre-Classic mask,
1100–800 B.C. Tlatilco, Mexico,
Mexico. Modeled, painted, and
perforated ceramic, 5.5 by
5.5 in. 23/5590

**Pre-Classic cylinder seal
representing Tezcatlipoca
(god of night and war) in
jaguar disguise,** 1000–600 B.C.
Temascalac, Puebla, Mexico.
Modeled and incised ceramic,
3.75 by 3.75 in. 23/9587

23/3131

24/1148

23/4953

22/9286

23/5590

23/9587

MESOAMERICA

Xochipala woman,
1100–500 B.C. Xochipala, Guerrero, Mexico. Modeled ceramic, 4.25 by 3.25 in. 24/1883

Chupícuaro female figure,
400–150 B.C. Chupícuaro, Guanajuato, Mexico. Modeled and painted ceramic, 12.5 by 6.5 in. 24/7600

Chupícuaro mother with baby, 400–150 B.C. Chupícuaro, Guanajuato, Mexico. Modeled, appliquéd, and painted ceramic, 4.75 by 3.25 in. 24/7606

Chupícuaro male figure,
400–150 B.C. Chupícuaro, Guanajuato, Mexico. Modeled, appliquéd, and painted ceramic, 5 by 3 in. 24/7620

Chupícuaro four-lobed bowl with faces, 400–150 B.C. Chupícuaro, Guanajuato, Mexico. Modeled and painted ceramic, 5 by 8.75 in. 23/1076

West Mexico female figurine,
400 B.C.–A.D. 200. Michoacán, Mexico. Modeled, appliquéd, and painted ceramic, 5.5 by 1.5 in. 24/1879

Shaft Tombs warrior,
300 B.C.–A.D. 600. Michoacán, Mexico. Modeled, painted (prefiring), and polished ceramic, 22.75 by 8.5 in. 21/6890

24/1883

24/7600

24/7606

24/7620

23/1076

21/6890

24/1879

Shaft Tombs model house,
300 B.C.–A.D. 600. Nayarit,
Mexico. Modeled and painted
ceramic, 12.75 by 9.5 in. 21/122

**Shaft Tombs tableau depict-
ing dancers and musicians,**
300 B.C.–A.D. 600. Nayarit,
Mexico. Modeled and painted
ceramic, 5.25 by 8.5 in. 23/2162

**Shaft Tombs mother with
baby,** 300 B.C.–A.D. 600.
Jalisco, Mexico. Modeled and
painted ceramic, 14.75 by 12 in.
RP1535

**Shaft Tombs jar in the form
of a man,** 300 B.C.–A.D. 600.
Buena Vista, Colima, Mexico.
Modeled and painted ceramic,
8.5 by 8 in. 22/5100

Shaft Tombs "clown" figure,
300 B.C.–A.D. 600. Colima,
Mexico. Modeled, painted (prefiring), and polished ceramic,
18 by 9 in. 22/5716

**Shaft Tombs scorpion-
shaped vessel,** 300 B.C.–A.D.
600. Colima, Mexico. Modeled,
painted (prefiring), and polished ceramic, 6.25 by
15.75 in. 24/5973

21/122

23/2162

22/5100

RP1535

24/5973

22/5716

MESOAMERICA

Shaft Tombs emaciated dog, 300 B.C.–A.D. 600. Colima, Mexico. Modeled, painted (prefiring), and polished ceramic, 13.5 by 9.25 in. 24/452

Shaft Tombs funerary mask, 300 B.C.–A.D. 600. Colima, Mexico. Modeled and painted ceramic, 9.75 by 8 in. 23/5498

Shaft Tombs female figure, 300 B.C.–A.D. 600. Nayarit, Mexico. Modeled and painted (prefiring) ceramic, 16.5 by 11 in. 23/2275

Shaft Tombs male figure, 300 B.C.–A.D. 600. Nayarit, Mexico. Modeled and painted (prefiring) ceramic, 20.75 by 11 in. 23/2276

Shaft Tombs mother and children, 300 B.C.–A.D. 600. Tecomán, Colima, Mexico. Modeled and painted ceramic, 8.25 by 6.5 in. 23/3868

Teotihuacán jar, A.D. 200–500. Toluca, Mexico, Mexico. Modeled, appliquéd, and incised ceramic, 12.25 by 14 in. 16/6067

24/452

23/5498

23/2275

23/2276

23/3868

16/6067

MESOAMERICA

Teotihuacán jar,
A.D. 250–450. Monte Albán,
Oaxaca, Mexico. Modeled
ceramic, 8.25 by 7 in. 23/3434

**Teotihuacán priest wearing
a Tláloc mask,** A.D. 250–450.
Teotihuacán, Mexico, Mexico.
Modeled, polished, and appliquéd ceramic, 7.75 by 5.25 in.
24/6989

**Teotihuacán cylindrical
tripod jar with cover,** A.D.
300–500. Teotihuacán, Mexico,
Mexico. Modeled, polished,
carved, and appliquéd ceramic,
9 by 6.25 in. 24/3383

**Teotihuacán cylindrical
tripod jar,** A.D. 300–500.
Teotihuacán, Mexico, Mexico.
Modeled, stuccoed, and painted
ceramic, 4.75 by 4.75 in.
22/9282

**Classic Teotihuacán-style
West Mexico double bowl,**
A.D. 500–600. Ahuejo, Michoacán, Mexico. Modeled, stuccoed, and painted ceramic,
2.5 by 11.25 in. 24/2975

**Maya tripod bowl depicting
a bird,** A.D. 1–650. Campeche,
Mexico. Modeled and painted
(pre- and postfiring) ceramic,
3.75 by 13.75 in. 24/7762

23/3434

24/6989

24/3383

22/9282

24/2975

24/7762

Maya polychrome tripod bowl, A.D. 300–650. Yucatán, Mexico. Modeled and painted ceramic, 3.5 by 13.5 in. 24/6499

Maya cylindrical ritual vase, A.D. 500–700. Campeche, Mexico. Modeled and painted ceramic, 6.25 by 4.75 in. 24/4089

Maya cylindrical ritual vase depicting priests, A.D. 500–700. Campeche, Mexico. Modeled and painted ceramic, 9.5 by 5.75 in. 24/4314

Jaina-style Maya flute, A.D. 400–700. Jaina Island, Campeche, Mexico. Modeled, appliquéd, and painted ceramic, 2 by 21.75 in. 24/1025

Jaina-style Maya whistle, A.D. 400–700. Guaymil, Campeche, Mexico. Modeled and painted ceramic, 10.5 by 4 in. 23/3781

Jaina-style Maya priest, A.D. 400–800. Jaina Island, Campeche, Mexico. Modeled, molded, painted, and appliquéd ceramic, 7.75 by 4 in. 23/8368

Jaina-style Maya figure of the ruler Halach Huinik, A.D. 400–800. Campeche, Mexico. Molded and painted ceramic, 11 by 6 in. 23/2216

24/4089

24/6499

24/4314

24/1025

23/3781

23/2216

23/8368

Jaina-style Maya drunkard, A.D. 400–800. Jaina Island, Campeche, Mexico. Modeled, appliquéd, and painted ceramic, 15 by 5.5 in. 23/2573

Jaina-style Maya weaver, A.D. 400–800. Jaina Island, Campeche, Mexico. Modeled and appliquéd ceramic, 6 by 6.25 in. 23/2865

Classic Central Veracruz female-figure rattle, A.D. 200–600. Nopiloa, Veracruz, Mexico. Modeled and painted ceramic, 9.25 by 8.25 in. 23/9576

Classic flute, A.D. 200–600. Nopiloa, Veracruz, Mexico. Molded and appliquéd ceramic, 1.75 by 13.5 in. 23/4048

Classic flute with monster figure, A.D. 200–600. Veracruz, Mexico. Modeled, molded, incised, and appliquéd ceramic, 6 by 12.5 in. 24/3352

Classic Central Veracruz trophy-head vessel, A.D. 300–600. Northern Veracruz, Mexico. Modeled, painted, and incised ceramic, 7 by 9.5 in. 24/3351

23/2573

23/2865

23/9576

23/4048

24/3352

24/3351

Remojadas male figure holding a bird, A.D. 300–600. Las Remojadas, Veracruz, Mexico. Modeled, appliquéd, and painted ceramic, 12.25 by 16 in. 23/6257

Remojadas female figure with baby, A.D. 300–600. Las Remojadas, Veracruz, Mexico. Modeled, appliquéd, and painted ceramic, 10.75 by 7.75 in. 23/9578

Remojadas seated noble or priest, A.D. 400–600. Huachín, Mexico. Modeled, appliquéd, and painted ceramic, 9.25 by 6.5 in. 24/3599

Remojadas female-figure whistle, A.D. 400–750. Dicha Tuerta, Veracruz, Mexico. Modeled and appliquéd ceramic, 12 by 9.5 in. 22/2310

Remojadas whistle depicting women on a swing, A.D. 400–750. Veracruz, Mexico. Modeled and painted ceramic, 6.25 by 8.5 in. 22/6374

23/6257

23/9578

24/3599

22/6374

22/2310

Remojadas female figurine holding fan, A.D. 400–750. Las Remojadas, Veracruz, Mexico. Modeled and painted (pre-and postfiring) ceramic, 27 by 19.5 in. 22/9277

Remojadas priest, A.D. 400–750. Las Remojadas, Veracruz, Mexico. Modeled, painted, and appliquéd ceramic, 24.5 by 9 in. 23/8555

Totonac footed bowl with bird design, A.D. 600–900. Juachín, Veracruz, Mexico. Modeled and painted (prefiring) ceramic, 4 by 10.75 in. 24/2721

Totonac rattle-base pedestal bowl depicting a crouching dog, A.D. 800–1200. Isla de Sacrificios, Veracruz, Mexico. Modeled and painted (prefiring) ceramic, 4 by 8.25 in. 23/653

Huastec loop-handle vessel depicting a jaguar and coyote, A.D. 800–1200. Pánuco, Veracruz, Mexico. Modeled, molded, and painted (prefiring) ceramic, 7 by 8.5 in. 24/1898

Paquimé vessel in the form of a woman, ca. A.D. 1200. Casas Grandes, Chihuahua, Mexico. Modeled and painted (prefiring) ceramic, 10.25 by 9.25 in. 6/582

Paquimé vessel in the form of a woman, ca. A.D. 1200. Casas Grandes, Chihuahua, Mexico. Modeled and painted (prefiring) ceramic, 6.5 by 13.75 in. 6/586

22/9277

23/8555

24/2721

23/653

24/1898

6/582

6/586

MESOAMERICA

Tarascan tripod bowl with rattle base, A.D. 1300–1521. Guererro, Mexico. Modeled and painted ceramic, 6 by 8.25 in. 23/7067

Tarascan pipe with jaguar-head rattle, A.D. 1300–1521. Tzintzuntzan, Michoacán, Mexico. Modeled and appliquéd ceramic, 2.5 by 21.25 in. 24/7623

Tarascan ritual jar with spout and long neck topped by a ring, A.D. 1300–1521. Tzintzuntzan, Michoacán, Mexico. Modeled and painted redware ceramic, 9.5 by 9 in. 24/7945

Post-Classic West Mexico female figure with characteristics of the male Xipe Tótec (god of spring and agriculture), A.D. 1300–1521. Colima, Mexico. Modeled, appliquéd, and painted (postfiring) ceramic, 29 by 14 in. 23/7831

Aztec mask, A.D. 1350–1521. Puebla, Mexico. Modeled, painted, and perforated ceramic, 3.5 by 3.75 in. 15/6338

Cholula-style Aztec cylindrical cup with pedestal base, A.D. 1300–1521. Cholula, Puebla, Mexico. Modeled, stuccoed, and painted (prefiring) ceramic, 8.25 by 4.5 in. 16/3393

23/7067

24/7623

24/7945

15/6338

23/7831

16/3393

Cholula-style Aztec male figure, A.D. 1350–1521. Puebla, Mexico. Modeled, painted (polychrome), and polished ceramic, 12 by 7 in. 23/6187

Cholula-style Aztec female figure, A.D. 1350–1521. Puebla, Mexico. Modeled, painted (polychrome), and polished ceramic, 13.5 by 7 in. 23/6188

Coatlalpanec-style Aztec globular drum, A.D. 1350–1521. Atlixco, Puebla, Mexico. Modeled, painted, appliquéd, polished, and pierced ceramic, 8.5 by 6.5 in. 4/9692

Post-Classic Maya censer, A.D. 1350–1521. Yucatán, Mexico. Modeled, painted, and polished ceramic, 8.75 by 6 in. 24/7783

***Incensario* (censer),** 2005. Made by Rubén Agurio Martínez Martínez (Nahua, b. 1945) and Eleazar Navarrete Ramírez (Nahua, b. 1951). Acatlán, Puebla, Mexico. Modeled ceramic, 2 by 1.75 in. 26/5279

Jar with handles and rope harness, 2005. Made by Rubén Agurio Martínez Martínez (Nahua, b. 1945) and Eleazar Navarrete Ramírez (Nahua, b. 1951). Acatlán, Puebla, Mexico. Modeled ceramic, rope, 4.5 by 4 in. 26/5274

23/6187

23/6188

4/9692

24/7783

26/5279

26/5274

MESOAMERICA

BRIDGING SPACE AND TIME

***Zuni olla* (water jar) depicting female dancers wearing *tablitas* (headdresses),** ca. 1850. Pueblo of Zuni, New Mexico. Modeled and painted ceramic, 11.5 by 14.75 in. 19/4356

Imprisoned Clown, ca. 1999. Made by Roxanne Swentzell (Santa Clara, b. 1962). Santa Clara Pueblo, New Mexico. Modeled and painted ceramic, 18.25 by 17 in. 26/4272

Tesuque double-spout pitcher, ca. 1890. Tesuque Pueblo, New Mexico. Modeled and painted Polychrome Two ceramic, 8.5 by 11.25 in. 6/201

Zuni cooking pot, A.D. 1400–1600. Hawikku, Zuni, New Mexico. Corrugated ceramic, 10 by 13 in. 10/6625

19/4356

6/201

26/4272

10/6625

Hopi jar, ca. A.D. 1400. Hawikku, Zuni, New Mexico. Modeled and painted ceramic, 8.75 by 14.25 in. 10/9676

Hopi-Tewa gourd-shaped canteen, ca. 1860. Hopi-Tewa Villages, Arizona. Modeled and painted Polacca Polychrome ceramic, 10 by 9.25 in. 19/4360

Sityatki Revival jar, ca. 1925. Made by Rachel Nampeyo (Hopi/Tewa, 1903–1985). Polacca Village, Arizona. Modeled and painted ceramic, 10.25 by 15.75 in. 21/2682

Jar, ca. 1959. Made by Maria Martinez (San Ildefonso, 1887–1980) and Popovi Da (San Ildefonso, 1921–1971). San Ildefonso Pueblo, New Mexico. Modeled and painted ceramic, 7.5 by 9.5 in. Indian Arts and Crafts Board Collection, Department of the Interior, at the National Museum of the American Indian. 25/8343

Seed jar, ca. 1985. Made by Grace Chino (Acoma, 1929–1994). Pueblo of Acoma, New Mexico. Modeled and painted ceramic, 9.25 by 10.25 in. 26/4159

Melon bowl, 1987. Made by Nancy Youngblood (Santa Clara, b. 1955). Santa Clara Pueblo, New Mexico. Modeled and polished blackware ceramic, 4.25 by 5.75 in. Indian Arts and Crafts Board Collection, Department of the Interior, at the National Museum of the American Indian. 25/5843

10/9676

19/4360

21/2682

25/8343

26/4159

25/5843

Hopi-Tewa storage jar, ca. 1880. Hopi-Tewa Villages, Arizona. Modeled and painted Polacca Polychrome ceramic, 20.5 by 18 in. 19/2701

Cochiti figurine, ca. 1880. Pueblo of Cochiti, New Mexico. Modeled and painted ceramic, 19 by 12.5 in. 19/6726

Acoma *olla* (water jar), ca. 1880. Pueblo of Acoma, New Mexico. Modeled and painted (polychrome) ceramic, 13 by 13 in. 23/4992

***Olla* (water jar),** ca. 1968. Made by Margaret Tafoya (Santa Clara, 1904–2001). Santa Clara Pueblo, New Mexico. Modeled and polished ceramic, 15.75 by 13.25 in. Indian Arts and Crafts Board Collection, Department of the Interior, at the National Museum of the American Indian. 25/9871

Zuni *olla* (water jar), ca. 1870. Pueblo of Zuni, New Mexico. Modeled and painted ceramic, 11.5 by 15.25 in. 22/7879

PUEBLO POTTERY AND CHANGE

Mogollon (Tularosa) bowl, A.D. 1050–1250. Tularosa Canyon, Catron County, New Mexico. Modeled, patterned-corrugated, and smudged ceramic, 7 by 10 in. 471

Tewa storage jar, ca. 1850. Santa Fe and Sandoval counties, New Mexico. Modeled and painted Powhoge Black-on-cream ceramic, 16.75 by 19 in. 5/3861

Dino Cube, 2004. Made by William Pacheco (Santo Domingo, b. 1975). Santo Domingo Pueblo, New Mexico. Modeled and painted ceramic, 9.25 by 9.25 in. 26/5271

19/2701

19/6726

23/4992

25/9871

22/7879

471

26/5271

5/3861

Cochiti singing-man pitcher, ca. 1890. Pueblo of Cochiti, New Mexico. Modeled and painted ceramic, 9 by 8.75 in. 7502

Tesuque devil figure, ca. 1880. Tesuque Pueblo, New Mexico. Modeled and painted ceramic, 8.75 by 5 in. 7528

Cochiti pitcher depicting a snail(?), ca. 1890. Pueblo of Cochiti, New Mexico. Modeled and painted ceramic, 7.5 by 7 in. 6/6819

Cochiti singing man, ca. 1890. Pueblo of Cochiti, New Mexico. Modeled and painted ceramic, 15.5 by 6.5 in. 6/6820

Cochiti duckling figure, ca. 1880. Pueblo of Cochiti, New Mexico. Modeled and painted ceramic, 6 by 8.5 in. 11/5015

Cochiti animal-human figurine, ca. 1880. Pueblo of Cochiti, New Mexico. Modeled and painted ceramic, 6.75 by 6.5 in. 16/9763

Cochiti animal-human figurine, ca. 1890. Pueblo of Cochiti, New Mexico. Modeled and painted ceramic, 10.75 by 7.75 in. 21/1134

Standing clown figure, 2005. Made by Lisa Holt (Cochiti, b. 1980) and Harlan Reano (Santo Domingo, b. 1978). Albuquerque, New Mexico. Modeled and painted ceramic, 20.5 by 15 in. 26/5237

7502

7528

6/6819

11/5015

6/6820

16/9763

26/5237

21/1134

Hopi-Tewa gourd-shaped canteen, ca. 1870. Hopi-Tewa Villages, Arizona. Modeled and painted Polacca Polychrome ceramic, 8.25 by 6 in. 4/742

Zia canteen, ca. 1890. Zia Pueblo, New Mexico. Modeled and painted ceramic, 5.5 by 7.25 in. 6/6828

Acoma canteen, ca. 1875. Pueblo of Acoma, New Mexico. Modeled and painted ceramic, 7.25 by 9 in. 16/1513

Canteen, 2003. Made by Nathan Begaye (Hopi/Navajo, b. 1959). Santa Fe, New Mexico. Modeled and painted ceramic, 8.5 by 8.5 in. 26/5269

CERAMICS AS AUTOBIOGRAPHIES

Ancestral Pueblo bowl, A.D. 875–1000. Pueblo Bonito, Chaco Canyon, New Mexico. Modeled and painted Red Mesa grayware ceramic, 4.5 by 9.5 in. 5/3048

Olla **(water jar),** ca. 1922. Made by Tsayutitsa (Zuni, ca. 1875–ca. 1955). Pueblo of Zuni, New Mexico. Modeled and painted ceramic, 9.5 by 12.75 in. 17/5988

San Ildefonso jar depicting a hunt, ca. 1890. San Ildefonso Pueblo, New Mexico. Modeled and painted ceramic, 8.75 by 9 in. 19/4337

Mimbres bowl, A.D. 1000–1150. Grant County, New Mexico. Modeled and painted ceramic, 5.5 by 11.75 in. 24/3196

4/742

6/6828

16/1513

26/5269

17/5988

5/3048

24/3196

19/4337

SOUTHWEST

Zuni jar, ca. A.D. 1400. Kechi-pauan, Zuni, New Mexico. Modeled, painted, and lead-glazed Kwakina Polychrome ceramic, 6.5 by 9.5 in. 12/3843

Cochiti storage jar, ca. 1890. Pueblo of Cochiti, New Mexico. Modeled and painted ceramic, 22 by 20.5 in. 21/6838

Zuni *olla* (water jar) depicting deer, ca. 1890. Pueblo of Zuni, New Mexico. Modeled and painted ceramic, 10 by 13.75 in. 22/7882

***Olla* (water jar),** ca. 1965. Made by Lucy M. Lewis (Acoma, 1895–1992). Pueblo of Acoma, New Mexico. Modeled and painted ceramic, 5 by 7.5 in. Indian Arts and Crafts Board Collection, Department of the Interior, at the National Museum of the American Indian. 25/5854

Jar, ca. 1985. Made by Jody Folwell (Santa Clara, b. 1942). Santa Clara Pueblo, New Mexico. Modeled, incised, and polished brownware ceramic, 6.75 by 9 in. 25/4761

12/3843

22/7882

21/6838

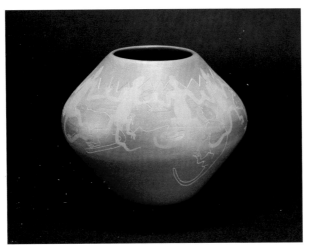

25/4761

25/5854

Vase, ca. 1975. Made by Tony Da (San Ildefonso, b. 1940). San Ildefonso Pueblo, New Mexico. Modeled and polished ceramic with duotone, sgraffito design, and inlaid shell, 12.5 by 9.75 in. Indian Arts and Crafts Board Collection, Department of the Interior, at the National Museum of the American Indian. 25/9870

Land of Entrapment, 1991. Made by Russell Sanchez (Santa Clara, b. 1966). San Ildefonso Pueblo, New Mexico. Modeled, painted, and incised ceramic, 7 by 5.75 in. 26/5061

Olla (water jar), 1991. Made by Lois Gutierrez de la Cruz (Pojoaque, b. 1949). Santa Clara Pueblo, New Mexico. Modeled and painted polychrome ceramic, 12 by 10.75 in. 26/5062

Osama Ken-Barbie, 2004. Made by Susan Folwell (Santa Clara, b. 1970) and Franzie Weldgen (b. 1972). Tucson, Arizona. Modeled and painted ceramic, 5.5 by 19.5 in. 26/4621

Stickball, 2004. Made by Diego Romero (Cochiti, b. 1964). Oklahoma. Modeled and painted ceramic, 6.25 by 12.25 in. 26/5249

25/9870

26/5061

26/5062

26/4621

26/5249

Plate, ca. 1990. Made by Christine McHorse (Navajo, b. 1949). Santa Fe, New Mexico. Modeled micaceous ceramic with raised embossed designs, 2 by 13.5 in. 26/4174

Plate, ca. 1970. Made by Margaret Tafoya (Santa Clara, 1904–2001). Santa Clara Pueblo, New Mexico. Modeled and polished ceramic, 2 by 13.34 in. 26/4282

Tile masks, ca. 2002. Made by Nora Naranjo-Morse (Santa Clara, b. 1953). Santa Clara Pueblo, New Mexico. Modeled and painted ceramic, largest: 7.75 by 4 in. 26/5270

Black-on-black plate, ca. 1930. Made by Tonita Roybal (San Ildefonso, 1892–1945) and Juan Cruz Roybal (San Ildefonso, 1896–1990). San Ildefonso Pueblo, New Mexico. Modeled and painted ceramic, 1.5 by 11.5 in. 24/7564

Plate, ca. 1957. Made by Maria Martinez (San Ildefonso, 1887–1980) and Popovi Da (San Ildefonso, 1921–1971). San Ildefonso Pueblo, New Mexico. Modeled and painted polychrome ceramic, 2.25 by 14.75 in. Indian Arts and Crafts Board Collection, Department of the Interior, at the National Museum of the American Indian. 25/8830

Black-on-black plate, 1930. Made by Maria Martinez (San Ildefonso, 1887–1980) and Julian Martinez (San Ildefonso, 1879–1943). San Ildefonso Pueblo, New Mexico. Modeled and painted ceramic, 1 by 9.75 in. 26/4234

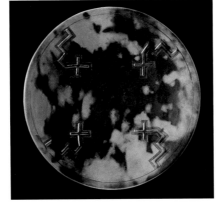

26/4174

26/4282

26/5270

24/7564

26/4234

25/8830

Santo Domingo storage jar, ca. 1880. Santo Domingo Pueblo, New Mexico. Modeled and painted ceramic, 17 by 17 in. 16/5876

Ancestral Pueblo storage or water jar, A.D. 1000–1100. Central New Mexico. Modeled and painted Socorro Black-on-white ceramic, 7 by 11 in. 5025

Storage jar, ca. 1910. Made by Florentino Montoya (San Ildefonso, 1862–1919) and Martina Montoya (Cochiti and San Ildefonso, 1857–1917). San Ildefonso Pueblo, New Mexico. Modeled and painted ceramic, 13.25 by 19 in. 11/5049

WORK BOWLS

Acoma dough bowl, ca. 1880. Pueblo of Acoma, New Mexico. Modeled and painted Acoma Polychrome ceramic, 9 by 16.5 in. 5/1087

Santo Domingo dough bowl, ca. 1880. Santo Domingo Pueblo, New Mexico. Modeled and painted ceramic, 11.75 by 19 in. 23/2472

5025

16/5876

11/5049

5/1087

23/2472

Laguna *olla* (water jar), ca. 1880. Laguna Pueblo, New Mexico. Modeled and painted ceramic, 12.5 by 14.25 in. 1/7841

Acoma double *olla* (water jar), ca. 1860. Pueblo of Acoma, New Mexico. Modeled and painted ceramic, 7.5 by 7 in. 8/7674

San Ildefonso *olla* (water jar), ca. 1910. Made by Tonita Roybal (San Ildefonso, 1892–1945); painting attributed to Crescencio Martinez (San Ildefonso, 1879–1918). San Ildefonso Pueblo, New Mexico. Modeled and painted ceramic, 11.25 by 12.75 in. 19/7294

Santa Clara rainbow jar or *olla* (water jar), ca. 1880. Santa Clara Pueblo, New Mexico. Modeled and polished ceramic, 12.75 by 14.75 in. 20/8459

1/7841

8/7674

19/7294

20/8459

Notes on the Collections

PAGE 44

24/8726 VALDIVIA FEMALE FIGURINE. Figurines from Valdivia are the most ancient ceramics known in the Western Hemisphere and probably are the equivalent of the Venus of Willendorf in the Old World. They are thought to be offerings to Pachamama, or Mother Earth, which may explain why they are found, broken, in sacred places. Complete figurines are very rare. R.M.

16/1971 CUPISNIQUE STIRRUP-SPOUT BOTTLE WITH MOUSE FIGURE. The rodent on the bottle appears to be a mouse, based on its body, staring look, and raised ears. The fact that the spout of the bottle leans against the animal's back suggests that it was made for an offering. This piece was probably once part of a larger assemblage. R.M.

24/6875 CUPISNIQUE STIRRUP-SPOUT BOTTLE IN THE FORM OF A WOMAN WASHING HER HAIR. In traditional Andean culture, urine is saved in special vessels. People wash their hair with it once a week, as part of a general cleansing of the body and spirit. Urine is also used as medicine, which is said to heal headaches and stomachaches. E.M.A.

24/3538 CUPISNIQUE BRIDGE-HANDLE BOTTLE WITH PARROT FIGURE. This vessel is an abstract representation of a root or tuber. The many varieties of parrots in the intermountain valleys were appreciated for their colored feathers. The parrot is represented in motion, with flapping wings and a standing crest, a posture parrots adopt when approaching their partner or nest. The wings and the back are decorated with incised abstract motifs. The sculptural representation of animals is very common in the Cupisnique style. R.M.

24/3535 CUPISNIQUE SNAKE-SHAPED, STIRRUP-SPOUT BOTTLE. The outer side of this curled snake's body is incised with circles and stair motifs, while the inner side presents a concentric rhombus. The Cupisnique style is characterized by a mastery of ceramic modeling with occasional use of incised lines and punctations. The feline and the snake, sometimes combined with the human body, were among the most common motifs. R.M.

24/1885 CUPISNIQUE MUSICIAN PLAYING PANPIPES. This musician is playing the traditional Andean *antara* (panpipes) with five tubes. He is seated with bent legs and wears a scarf and a headdress decorated with punctated lines and red cinnabar spots. Andean music is pentatonic, with the five tubes of the panpipe rendering the five notes of the pentatonic scale. R.M.

24/4326 CHORRERA BOWL DEPICTING A DEAD MAN. This seated man wears a brown hat and is wrapped in a mantel richly decorated with concentric rhombus designs. His mouth is sealed by a peg, indicating that he is dead. This bowl must thus have been used to contain liquid for a funerary ceremony. R.M.

PAGE 45

23/8375 PARACAS FELINE-SHAPED, BRIDGE-HANDLE BOTTLE. This feline, called *titi* in Aymara and *osgollu* in Quechua, lives among the rocks of the ocean shore and is an important animal in Andean mythology. The vessel itself was used for offerings. The Paracas style, which developed on the southern coast of Peru during the Formative period (1400–100 B.C.), is known for its post-firing painting technique. R.M.

11/2810 NAZCA DOUBLE-SPOUT-AND-BRIDGE BOTTLE DEPICTING CHILE PEPPERS. In the early stages of Nazca culture, artists represented plants and animals in a realistic style, while in later periods, the style became more abstract and barely recognizable. This piece belongs to the early style called Monumental Nazca. R.M.

11/2597 NAZCA STIRRUP-SPOUT BOTTLE IN THE FORM OF A BURDEN BEARER. This man, who wears a hat and face paint, carries a huge burden. There were no draft animals in the Andes, except for the llama in the high mountains. Since llamas can only carry loads weighing up to 90 pounds, people carried heavier burdens of up to 180 pounds. R.M.

11/2807 NAZCA CANTEEN DEPICTING WATER AND FISH. One side of this vessel exhibits concentric circles, which represent water or rain in Andean symbolism, and the other shows fishes in movement. This vessel comes from the coast and must be related to the sea and rain. R.M.

15/9414 NAZCA TRUMPET. The body of this trumpet is decorated with a figurative scene: thin personages seen from the back alternate with two larger figures seen from the front. The latter wear masks and hold authority sticks ending in a bird's head. The Nazca style developed on the southern coast of Peru and is characterized by the high quality of its polychrome ceramics, which are adorned with naturalistic and abstract motifs. R.M.

PAGE 46

1/9024 NAZCA DRUM. The body of this drum has three sections. The central section is decorated with a painted panel representing drumsticks and joyful people who may be singing. Ceramic drums covered with deerskin were very common in the Nazca style. R.M.

11/2516 NAZCA CUP DEPICTING WARRIORS DANCING. The very schematic painting on this cup depicts dancing soldiers wearing bi-pointed headdresses and slings and whips attached to their waists. The artist suggests transformation of soldiers into powerful warriors. R.M.

11/2503 NAZCA CYLINDRICAL CUP DEPICTING TROPHY HEADS AND A WINGED BEING. This cup is richly decorated: the upper register represents stair motifs; the lower a succession of trophy heads; and the middle a stylized representation of a winged personage. This vessel is in the late phase of the Nazca style. R.M.

11/2507 NAZCA CYLINDRICAL CUP DEPICTING FISH AND CENTIPEDES. The cup is decorated by an upper and a lower band of stylized fish motifs on a white background and, in the middle register, by a series of interlocked centipede representations which alternate in two different patterns. R.M.

11/2763 NAZCA SPIRAL-RIDGE CUP DEPICTING WINGED BEINGS. The flying beings depicted on the upper part of this vessel have condor or falcon wings, with feathers ending in snake heads, and legs decorated with little human heads. This is a good example of Nazca mythological representation of humans being transformed into supernatural creatures. R.M.

211/2891 NAZCA GLOBULAR POT DE-PICTING CONDORS AND PENGUINS. Each side of the vessel exhibits a stylized condor, with feathers that end in a snake's head with a long tongue. Three penguins are depicted between these two condors. In Andean mythology the snake is thought to come from the condor's feathers. R.M.

11/2781 NAZCA DOUBLE-SPOUT-AND-BRIDGE BOTTLE. The upper part of this vessel bears a representation of two grotesque figures: the body with its legs and arms is clearly visible; the face has an open mouth from which protrudes a long tongue that ends in a centipede form and a succession of heads. A lower band on the bottle is decorated with a series of identical human faces. R.M.

PAGE 47

11/2566 NAZCA DOUBLE-SPOUT-AND-BRIDGE BOTTLE IN THE FORM OF A SNAKE. The body of the snake is deco-rated with mythological characters: human beings, the condor, the feline, and the snake. R.M.

11/2798 NAZCA GLOBULAR JAR. This jar probably depicts a triumphant warrior with his trophy head and the knife he used to take it. He wears a necklace, and his clothes are decorated with a curvilinear rope. R.M.

23/6189 MOCHE TOAD-SHAPED, STIRRUP-SPOUT BOTTLE. This three-dimensional representation is a very realistic evocation of a toad in motion. The Moche style is character-ized by its *huacos retratos* (ceramic portraits). R.M.

5/1890 MOCHE STIRRUP-SPOUT BOTTLE IN THE FORM OF A SQUATTING MAN. This man is wearing a loincloth and a hat and has decorative scarifications on his face representing birds and abstract motifs. He seems to be sad or ill. R.M.

24/7645 MOCHE STIRRUP-SPOUT BOTTLE IN THE FORM OF A TROPHY HEAD. This trophy's face is deco-rated in four quadrants, alternatively painted red and white, to symbolize the two-part structure of the universe, with complementary sides that unite in a common center. R.M.

PAGE 48

24/7955 MOCHE STIRRUP-SPOUT BOTTLE IN THE FORM OF A SEATED NOBLEMAN. This is an effigy of a sitting leader, perhaps a priest or a ruler, as indicated by his turban, earplugs, and the bicolored broad collar, all insignia of high rank. R.M.

9/7245 MOCHE PORTRAIT CUP. This *huaco retrato* (ceramic portrait) cup, used for sacrificial purposes, repro-duces the face of an actual person. A series of these portraits might be made of a person at different ages. Use of molds allowed these portraits to be reproduced in great numbers. R.M.

12/9889 MOCHE WHISTLE IN THE FORM OF A PACAY OR HUAVA FRUIT (INGA FEUILLEI). The pacay tree, domesti-cated in the Andes, produces fruit with edible white pulp surrounding large black seeds. R.M.

19/9297 MOCHE WHISTLE IN THE FORM OF A TILLANDSIA PLANT (SPANISH MOSS). Tillandsia is an epiphyte, or "air plant," that grows in the Perúvian desert. It belongs to the Bromeliaceae family and is known as Spanish moss or ball moss. Because water collects between its leaves, it is used by both humans and animals. The dried plant is also consumed and cooked. In the desert's loneliness, tillandsias are the only plants that grow in little colonies. R.M.

22/3546 MOCHE JAR IN THE FORM OF A MUSICIAN PLAYING A DRUM. The seated musician holds a drum in one hand and a drumstick in the other. The folded cloth attached to his waist may contain coca leaves or food. R.M.

PAGE 49

24/3816 MOCHE GLOBULAR BOTTLE WITH RITUAL REPRESENTATIONS. Mod-eled dogs top the shoulders of this vessel, while stylized painted designs cover each side of the bottle. On the upper level, two shamans present an offering, and in the lower part, a central personage is being sacrificed by two others. The complex decoration of this bottle was created using a master mold and painting with a fine slip. R.M.

23/7006 RECUAY PITCHER WITH FELINE FIGURE. The snout and fur of the ani-mal at the top of this vessel suggest it is feline, possibly a puma. However, its eyes, ears, tail, and hooves resemble those of a llama. The bottom of the vessel presents a frieze of stylized humans in profile, with large heads and small arms and legs. R.M.

23/8938 VICUS STIRRUP-SPOUT BOTTLE. One man is massaging the back of his companion. This type of healing func-tions by the transmission of energy. Both men are dressed in black-and-white clothes and have long hair. R.M.

24/6659 LA TOLITA DRUM WITH THREE FACES. This drum is decorated with three modeled human faces: two diametrically opposed large faces with a third, smaller one in between. The red-painted faces have deep wrinkles at the sides of their mouths and wear earrings, *narigueras* (nose ornaments), and headbands. Ceramic drums covered with deerskin were used in important feasts and ceremonies. R.M.

24/6607 GUANGALA WHISTLE. This clay figure exhibits finely incised decora-tions which depict the personage's clothing, which including a headdress, jacket, and blanket held by a cord at the waist. R.M.

24/462 BAHÍA FIGURE OF A CROSS-LEGGED MAN. This richly dressed man, possibly a shaman, wears an elaborate headdress, ear ornaments, and a sea lion canine-tooth collar. He seems to be consuming something like coca, since he holds rolled leaves in his right hand and a vessel used to store lime in the other. R.M.

PAGE 50

1/6004 BAHÍA MUSICIAN PLAYING PAN-PIPES. This musician is richly dressed in a headdress, cloak, *nariguera* (nose ornament), and loincloth. He is play-ing panpipes, called *siku* in Quechua and *antara* in Aymara. Ecuador's coastal tradition of making human effigies in clay originated at Valdivia (3500 B.C.) and lasted until the arrival of Europeans. R.M.

1/6272 BAHÍA HEALER OR PRIEST. This richly dressed man, who sits on an authority seat, is a high-status person, probably a priest, shaman, or chief. He wears a loincloth, headdress, and *nariguera* (nose ornament) and holds an authority bracelet in his left hand. His body is decorated with scarifications of parallel and horizon-tal lines. R.M.

23/9930 BAHÍA FEMALE FIGURINE. This figurine has a headdress, coffee-grain eyes, and prominent lips. The upper part of her body and her feet are painted red. These figurines were made for offerings or could also be part of a *curandero's* (healer's) paraphernalia. R.M.

24/3220 BAHÍA DOUBLE-LOBED WHISTLING BOTTLE WITH SHAMAN FIGURINE. This figurine, richly dressed and adorned, sits on a ritual seat. He is identified as a shaman because he holds a serpent in each hand. The snake symbolizes life and energy, which is why shamans wear snake amulets or snake skins. R.M.

24/4823 JAMA-COAQUE MALE-FIGURE WHISTLE. This high-status man wears a long tunic with a broad (beaded?) collar, a huge headdress, and jewelry, including a *nariguera* (nose orna-ment), labret, and bracelets. In real life, the large whistle would sound as the wind blows; on this piece, the whistle can be played. This man appears to be giving orders, making a speech, or worshipping. R.M.

24/4450 TIWANAKU PEDESTAL-BASED CENSER WITH CONDOR. In the Andean conception of the world there are three levels: the sky, the earth, and the underworld. The condor represents the sky, and people pay tribute to him for he is the only animal capable of contacting the celestial world spirits. Because of this, the condor is very sacred, and its feathers can only be handled by priests. E.M.A.

20/6313 TIWANAKU PEDESTAL-BASED CENSER WITH JAGUAR. In Andean mythology, the jaguar is frequently associated with the condor and the serpent. They can be represented individually, or they can be combined with one another to produce a power-ful animal that accumulates all their strengths. An abstract representation of the condor decorates both sides of this vessel's body. R.M.

PAGE 51

20/6317 TIWANAKU BOTTLE DEPICTING A LLAMA OR ALPACA. The animal's bent neck and lowered ears on this expres-sive bottle suggest that it represents a newborn camelid. However, the large body size may indicate a pregnant female ready to give birth. This type of vessel was intended for offerings. R.M.

24/3817 WARI DOUBLE-SPOUT-AND-BRIDGE BOTTLE DEPICTING CONDORS. Both sides of this bottle's upper body depict two anthropomorphic condors flying amid circular motifs that rep-resent the eyes of the sky. In Andean mythology, the sky is said to have eyes flying in space. R.M.

23/1070 WARI BOTTLE. Here, a boa constrictor is wrapped around a man, whose face is represented on the bot-tle's spout. Sophisticated polychrome motifs are drawn on the snake's body: the face of the traditional divinity called Wiraqocha alternates with depictions of feline faces. R.M.

24/6655 PANZALEO CANTEEN IN THE FORM OF A PREGNANT WOMAN. This woman, with her hands on her belly, is ready to give birth. The practice of painting the face with ocher, as shown on this vessel, is still practiced during birthing rites in some modern-day communities. These female figurines were used as amulets in offering rituals intended for Pachamama (Mother Earth). R.M.

3/360 TUZA TRIPLE-BODY VESSEL WITH BASKET HANDLE. In Andean thought, the world has three levels: the sky, the earth, and the underworld. This vessel may have been used to make offerings to all these levels by placement of white *chicha* (maize beer), dark *chicha*, and pure water in its respective compartments. E.M.A.

3/875 TUZA-PIARTAL WHISTLE IN THE FORM OF A LAND SNAIL. The piece, which has a hollow space for the circulation of air, was used as a whistle. The hole on one end allowed it to be worn on a string around the neck. Felines are depicted on the whistle's light slip: one is giving birth, another is mating, and others are running or holding plants. R.M.

PAGE 52

23/7003 PIARTAL FOOTED PLATE DEPICTING DANCERS. This plate's interior painting represents a circle of eleven people holding hands, with the Andean cross, or *chacana*, in the center. The chacana serves as an entrance to the spiritual world. Plates, known as *uku* in Quechua, are used to hold food or burn incense during rituals. This *uku* probably depicts a communal feast held involving a spiritual connection with the chacana symbol. R.M.

3/324 CAPULI FOOTED PLATE. The inside of this plate is decorated with four alternating images of the sun and the moon. This symbolism indicates that the plate was made to arrange offerings for the gods. R.M.

11/1359 LAMBAYEQUE BRIDGE-HANDLE WHISTLING BOTTLE DEPICTING MAIZE DEITY. One side of this bottle's handle depicts the god of maize with his impressive headdress of a bundle of corncobs. Maize remains a sacred plant in Andean cosmology and this bottle depicts a traditional celebration in honor of Mama Sara (the corn goddess), which still takes place during the May harvest. On this occasion, girls used to wear headdresses made of corncobs like that on this pot. R.M.

23/6883 CHIMÚ STIRRUP-SPOUT BOTTLE IN THE FORM OF A DUCK. This bottle shows a marine duck swimming with its head raised to catch a fish. The modeled monkey applied to the spout is characteristic of Chimú stirrup-spout vessels. The Chimú state developed on the northern coast of Peru before the Inka Empire. Chimú potters mass-produced ceramics using molds. R.M.

15/1457 CHIMÚ BOTTLE IN THE FORM OF A *LOSHI* (SQUASH). At least fifteen cucurbit varieties, most of them edible, are native to the Andes. Some have picturesque forms resembling a snake or a bird. R.M.

PAGE 53

19/9298 CASMA BOTTLE IN THE FORM OF *PEPINOS* OR *KACHUM* (MELON PEARS). This four-bodied bottle has four little handles representing the fruits' stems. Each fruit is decorated by red and white lines that realistic portray the pepino. This fruit is domesticated in the Andean region. R.M.

14/5496 CHUQUIBAMBA PITCHER DEPICTING LLAMAS. The body of this red-slipped vessel is painted with llamas all running in the same direction, while the rim is exhibits a black zigzagging line. The Puquina people who made this vessel lived around Lake Titicaca and were conquered by the Inka. R.M.

14/3673 INKA DOUBLE-CHAMBERED BOTTLE WITH MAN AND LLAMA FIGURES. This man carries an *arybal* (jar) on his back and pulls a reluctant llama with a rope. The animal is probably on its way to be sacrificed as part of a ritual; the man may be a shaman. R.M.

20/6477 INKA VESSEL DEPICTING A MAN CARRYING AN *ARYBALO* (JAR). This man wears a long headdress, which has the same painted decoration as his arybal, and his face is painted in white and black. This piece was produced for ritual purposes. R.M.

16/4835 INKA *PAQCHA* (RITUAL VESSEL) DEPICTING A LLAMA HEAD WITH *ARYBALO* (JAR) ON TOP. This type of vessel, used to pour water in Inka rituals, is still used in pastoral ceremonies. The llama is recognizable by its elongated head and snout; the arybal, a signature vessel of the Inka state, is decorated on its front with *quipus*, knotted cords used for counting animals. The Inka state standardized the production of goods such as ceramics and textiles. R.M.

20/6341 INKA *QOCHA* (RITUAL VESSEL). The concentric black lines on the interior of this typical Inka qocha represent waves. The bowl's rim used to have a duck effigy, which is now broken off; only its stylized legs are preserved. R.M.

20/6347 INKA MINIATURE VESSEL. The decoration painted on one side of this vessel resembles a textile. The symmetry of the design reflects the rigorous Inka concept of duality: the two outer columns represent stylized ferns, and the central columns exhibit alternating geometrical patterns. This piece is made in Classic Inka style. R.M.

PAGE 54

16/1060 CHANCAY JAR. These types of representations are called "chinas," because of the shape of their eyes. Body painting is visible on the face, hands, and arms. Vessels with face-spouts are usually found in pairs and were very popular in the Chancay style common on the central coast of Peru. R.M.

1/1596 CHIMBORAZO PEDESTAL PLATE. This plate reflects mestizo ceramic production. Although the pedestal plate (*compotera*) is a Native form, it has been decorated with the western technique of glazing. The green color is obtained by using copper oxide. R.M.

6/3307 AYMARA RING-SHAPED *PAQCHA* (RITUAL VESSEL) WITH ANIMAL HEADS. The paqcha is used for August rituals linked to the herds. Water or *chicha* (maize beer) is put in the jar through its spout and then poured onto the ground through the animals' heads. R.M.

20/6386 QUECHUA MEDICINAL OR CEREMONIAL CUP. Only one of the four straws, or *bombillas*, is open and connected to the cup; the others are decorative and nonfunctional. By using four straws, the potter symbolized the four directions. The black and white designs on the cup's body represent plants. R.M.

PAGE 55

26/5293 *QERO* (RITUAL VESSEL), made by Exaltación Mamani Amaro (Quechua) and Irma Rodríguez Moroco (Quechua). Qeros are traditional Andean drinking vessels. They are also used to collect the blood of sacrificial llamas and to make offerings of *chicha*, a fermented corn drink. Traditionally made of wood, today many qeros are made of pottery. They are still used by shamans during healing rituals and agricultural ceremonies. T.B.A.

26/5272 FRUIT PLATE, made by Exaltación Mamani Amaro (Quechua) and Irma Rodríguez Moroco (Quechua). The spider and bird designs used here are drawn from the Nazca lines, massive earthworks built between 200 B.C. and A.D. 600 in coastal Peru. Today's Quechua potters consciously embrace ancient designs in their work to reference their ancestral traditions.

26/5289 LIDDED BOWLS, made by Exaltación Mamani Amaro (Quechua) and Irma Rodríguez Moroco (Quechua). These bowls are perfect examples of how pottery has changed and stayed the same over time. Although these bowls were made to cater to tourists' tastes, the artists still try to use their parents' and grandparents' ways when making pottery. T.B.A.

RIVERS OF INTERACTION: THE CERAMICS OF EASTERN NORTH AMERICA

PAGE 57

On "Archaeological Cultures"

In analyzing what Native people of the past left behind, archaeologists have developed cultural frameworks and chronologies based on similarities and differences in archaeological remains and the behaviors they are believed to encode. Where evidence from a particular archaeological site or set of sites may identify people as culturally or temporally distinct from others, archaeologists use the original site name or another feature to refer to that complex of identifiable traits. However, we must remain mindful that such archaeologically defined "cultures" do not reflect what people would have called themselves, nor do they represent individual societies in the way a specific term such as "Seneca" might. For example, the "Owasco culture" of New York (A.D. 1000–1300) is considered to be ancestral to all five historic Iroquois tribes, thus archaeological cultures can often be far more encompassing than what we consider tribes or cultures today. A.M.

Underwater Panther and Great Serpent

Underwater Panther and Great Serpent were important Mississippian supernatural Underworld beings and may represent the same figure depicted in different ways. These incarnations vary in their cat- or snake-like features along with the addition of wings, horns, and talons. This terrifying creature, with its combined attributes of several powerful animals, resided in a cave with an underwater entrance. While some traditions describe the Great Serpent as an evil power, others credit it with a role in the great Creation. The Great Serpent is also said to guard the entrance to a great lodge where the most powerful animal doctors safeguard the knowledge of the universe. Worthy humans seeking that knowledge might be allowed to enter and be instructed in ceremonies that could be taken back to the Terrestrial World to better the lives of the people. T.E.E.

Woodpeckers and Warriors

Within the schema of the four cardinal directions and Native oral traditions, Morning Star and the Sun are associated with the East and with masculine powers, ruling over war and the hunt. Evening Star and Moon are associated with the West and feminine powers, especially fertility: Evening Star maintains a beautiful garden where the corn is always ripe and game is plentiful.

In traditional depictions, Morning Star has a fiery red crest symbolizing his strength, anger, and love of war. He drives the other stars toward the west and from the sky each morning. Because woodpeckers also have fiery red crests, they became the earthly symbol of the Morning Star and were depicted as such on stone pipes, shell cups, and weapons, as well as ceramics. In contemporary Native American dances, Morning Star and warrior status are represented by woodpecker feathers and roach headdresses made of red-dyed deer hair. T.E.E.

PAGE 58

Caddoan Bottles

The Caddoans were a group of tribes living in scattered farming communities along the rivers of southeastern Oklahoma, southwestern Arkansas, northwestern Louisiana, and northeastern Texas. Their members spoke closely related languages of the Caddoan language family. Archaeologically, they emerged as a cultural group after A.D. 800, interacting with but distinct from Mississippian peoples. Their location put them in a unique position to supply products such as salt, dried buffalo meat, and hides from their own area and the neighboring Plains to population centers along the Mississippi. Through this trade, the Caddoans accumulated abundant prestige goods such as those excavated at the Spiro Mounds site on the Arkansas River, one of their trading and ceremonial centers. Physically separated from the Mississippians and their internal conflicts, the Caddoans lived with little stress and abundant food, fostering an atmosphere in which artistic talent could flourish. Caddoan ceramics are thought by many to be the most beautiful in eastern North America.

Situated between Mississippian centers and Mexico, the Caddoans were often the first to take up new ideas in ceramics flowing out of Mexico, often a century or more before the same ideas reached the lower Mississippi Valley. Bottles are one such innovation, appearing in Caddoan areas after A.D. 900 and the lower Mississippi almost 300 years later.

Caddoan potters applied the full range of their decorative techniques to bottles, either incising patterns in the clay while it was still wet or engraving polished brown or black bottles with fine lines after they were fired and rubbing red or white pigment into the designs. Contemporary Caddo potter Jereldine Redcorn honors these ancestral forms and decorative techniques in her work. T.E.E.

PAGE 59

Cooking Pots

Early cooking pots had straight sides and slightly pointed bases. However, as Native people shifted to rely more on corn, beans, and other cultivated crops, potters developed new forms better suited to slow-cooking these foods, specifically globular bodies and narrower rims. Because these pots were used daily and were a focal point of the family hearth and meals, potters took special care in making them both durable and beautiful. A.M.

Effigy Pipes

Although cooking pots and other vessels were the most common forms, ceramic pipes and pottery figures were made by Native people. Clay pipes may have been fashioned by men and women and were probably used for casual smoking of herbal mixtures, unlike the elaborate stone pipes that were more likely used for prayer and communal rituals involving tobacco. Effigies on pipes, whether animal or human, were positioned to face the smoker. A.M.

PAGE 60

Tripod Bottles

Tripod bottles with hollow, bulbous feet, an innovation from Mexico, reached Caddoan peoples after A.D. 1200. In some cases, as in the example here from Le Flore County, Oklahoma, potters experimented with the idea to the point of almost eliminating the bottle's body altogether and simply connecting the feet to the neck. The possibilities of the tripod bottle were taken even further with the famous Triune Vessel, excavated in Tennessee in 1819. Despite its provenance, this bottle was probably made in the southeastern corner of Missouri, where human representations such as "head pots" and Janus bottles were more common. T.E.E.

Weather, Wind, and Water

In addition to supernatural figures associated with the Southeastern Ceremonial Complex, Mississippian iconography also included representations of animals and abstract symbols such as swirls, spirals, and swastikas. Many of these motifs, including water animals, have been interpreted as evidence of fertility symbolism that co-existed with other religious or spiritual practices. These symbols may also have related to the cultivation or placation of the forces of weather, wind, and water—all critical to the success of the crops on which these agricultural societies depended. A.M.

PAGE 61

The Big Bone Bank Site, Posey County, Indiana

Located on the banks of the Wabash River near its confluence with the Ohio at the southwestern tip of Indiana, the Big Bone Bank site, as its name suggests, was marked by human bones and grave goods which eroded out of more than 800 meters of riverbank. Originally recorded in 1806, Bone Bank saw its first excavation in 1828, and over the years it became a popular destination for local residents seeking "antiquities." One resident sold his collection of 600 Bone Bank objects to the Museum of the American Indian in 1916. By the early twentieth century, the Bone Bank cemeteries had all washed away, and the related village site was largely destroyed. Between 2000 and 2003, Indiana University performed rescue excavations at what little remains of the site.

Bone Bank was occupied around A.D. 1400, a time of population shifts and sociopolitical upheaval at this northern edge of the great Mississippian chiefdoms. Though seemingly remote, Bone Bank's riverine location fostered contact with these Mississippian populations, and some Bone Bank ceramics show unmistakable connections with peoples to the south and southeast. The shell-shaped bowl implies either journeys to the Gulf of Mexico or long-distance trade with people living there, while the ogee-motif bottle suggests relationships with Moundville. Two-faced "Janus" bottles are typical of those found in southeastern Missouri, and the bowl with elaborately coiffed human head is reminiscent of Mexican depictions of the corn god.

Because the integrity of the site was so damaged over time, we may never know whether Bone Bank's southern connections came from trade or from an influx of people who moved

there from collapsing Mississippian chiefdoms. If the latter, the newcomer may have established themselves as an elite class ruling over the local population, who made the very different everyday pottery also found at the site. P.L.N.

Clarence Bloomfield Moore (1852–1936): Pioneering Archaeologist or Insatiable Grave Robber?

From 1891 to 1918, Clarence Moore spent almost every winter navigating the rivers and coasts of the South in his paddlewheel steamboat, *Gopher*. But he wasn't on a pleasure cruise—he was on the hunt for Indian mounds. Given the importance of water transport to Native travel, Moore knew that the most significant mounds and villages were close to shore. All he need do was tie the Gopher to a convenient riverbank and send his crew out to dig, and he would be rewarded with a haul of beautiful artifacts—almost all of them from Indian graves. Therein lies the dilemma of Clarence Moore.

Although not a trained archaeologist, Moore was sponsored by the Academy of Natural Sciences of Philadelphia (where he deposited most of his collection) and corresponded with professionals at many institutions, including the Smithsonian. His fieldwork met the standards of his day: He kept field notebooks; he placed his carefully cataloged collections in public museums; and most important (and astonishing), he published his results in more than fifty scholarly papers, many of them beautifully illustrated monographs that he personally financed. These publications laid the groundwork for later studies and often constitute our only record of sites never revisited or since destroyed.

Nevertheless, Moore was specifically searching for graves because they held exhibit-quality objects—funerary offerings placed with the dead. He would probe a mound with an iron rod to locate burials. If unsuccessful, he sailed on; if successful, he spent a few days digging up as many graves as possible, sometimes destroying the site in the process. Moore sent those skeletons "worth saving" to the Army Medical Museum and other repositories, but he discarded most remains, because they disintegrated or were damaged on excavation.

Independently wealthy, Moore wasn't in it for the money; he wanted recognition as a gentleman scholar in the Victorian mold. In 1929, the Academy of Natural Sciences, needing more space for its zoological exhibits, secretly sold more than 20,000 of Moore's artifacts to the Museum of the American Indian.

Today, these objects are considered some of NMAI's "treasures," for it is through Moore's collections from Florida, Georgia, South Carolina, Tennessee, Kentucky, Alabama, Mississippi, Louisiana, and Arkansas that the artistry of southeastern Native cultures came to be appreciated. More than thirty vessels in this book come from Moore's excavations (look for catalogue numbers beginning with 17). Yet they leave unanswered the question, Was Moore's fieldwork worth it? P.L.N.

PAGE 62

17/4454 LATE WOODLAND (WEEDEN ISLAND CULTURE) FOOTED JAR. Sand-tempered and red-painted Weeden Island ceramics are usually associated with the Gulf Coast of Florida. However, this jar comes from the Chattahoochee River, Georgia. It may represent a potter copying the Weeden Island style or a trading relationship with the Florida coast. T.E.E.

17/3870 LATE WOODLAND (WEEDEN ISLAND CULTURE) JAR WITH SCALLOPED RIM. Crystal River on the Gulf Coast of Florida north of Tampa Bay was occupied for 1,500 years. Artifacts from this site demonstrate trading relationships with Late Woodland Period Hopewell peoples and others to the north and west. T.E.E.

17/1441 CADDOAN SQUARED BOTTLE. The body of this early Caddoan bottle is distinguished by a squared-off quartered form superimposed on a rounded base. This squared-off form is readily apparent when the bottle is turned upside down as it would have been in use. T.E.E.

17/4639 CADDOAN CASTELLATED JAR WITH STRAP HANDLES. This jar is a half step between typical cord-marked Woodlands vessels and more elaborate Late Mississippian ceramics. It retains the typical Woodlands shape but exhibits additional decoration and a flat Caddoan bottom. Clarence Moore, who excavated it, called it a cooking pot; it certainly is a fancy one. T.E.E.

PAGE 63

17/3715 CADDOAN BOTTLE. The swirl design on this red bottle was engraved into the surface of the clay after the vessel was fired. T.E.E.

17/1398 LATE MISSISSIPPIAN BOTTLE. The bottle shape and red-and-white decoration occur together on ceramics in the Mississippi Valley just before the De Soto entrada of 1539–43. The white pigment used to create the swirl design probably came from galena (lead ore) mined in the tri-state area of Oklahoma, Kansas, and Missouri. T.E.E.

17/4224 LATE MISSISSIPPIAN GLOBULAR BOTTLE. The swirl design on this bottle from the St. Francis River valley was incised into the clay' surface while it was still wet. Swirl designs are common throughout the Mississippian world. T.E.E.

17/4489 GUALE JAR. Jars with stamped decoration like this were made on the Georgia coast for 1,500 years. Potters pressed carved wooden or ceramic stamps into the wet clay of unfired vessels to produce this surface texture. Stamps have been found in archaeological excavations. P.L.N.

PAGE 64

Late Mississippian Vessels

12/6549 LATE MISSISSIPPIAN BOTTLE. This vessel was excavated at Carden Bottom, a Caddoan trading center on the Arkansas River. It represents an abstraction of the head and exaggerated open mouth of a baby bird. The raised markings inside the mouth are specific to various bird species and indicate the depth of knowledge that these people had of the natural world in which they lived. T.E.E.

5/2981 LATE MISSISSIPPIAN JAR. This vessel is a lifelike representation of an honored deceased warrior. Incised facial markings show the tattoos or scarification the warrior had in life. Ear piercings and wear patterns indicate that this pot was decorated and used for a time before burial. The eye decoration, sometimes called a grappling-hook design, actually resembles the spread wings of a large bird. T.E.E.

5/1082 LATE MISSISSIPPIAN BOTTLE. The negative painted design on this bottle represents the sun. For some southeastern peoples, the sun was the principal god. Visitors to the Natchez of Louisiana in the early eighteenth century tell us that their paramount chief was called "Great Sun." T.E.E.

7387 LATE MISSISSIPPIAN BOTTLE IN THE FORM OF A HUMAN LEG TROPHY WITH PROTRUDING FEMUR. The exposed femur on this "hooded bottle" suggests it depicts a severed human leg, perhaps a trophy taken in war, since warfare was endemic in Mississippian society. Enemy warriors who died bravely were often dismembered so their spirits would not be encountered again in the next life. T.E.E.

Caddoan Vessels

6641 CADDOAN SPHERICAL SEED JAR. The shape of this vessel, one of eighteen found in a single mound, suggests it was used to store seeds. With its mouth stoppered by a corncob, its contents were effectively protected from rodents. Great numbers of similar jars washed out from Watermelon Island on the Arkansas River, corroborating the supposition that they were used for storage. T.E.E.

PAGE 65

New England and Mid-Atlantic Vessels

5/3482 LATE WOODLAND CORNCOB-SHAPED JAR. Late Woodland peoples of southeastern New England made carefully decorated ceramics, including examples like this small vessel. Its intended use is unknown, but it may once have had a corncob stopper and been used to hold salt or carry medicine. A.M.

22/446 SUSQUEHANNOCK JAR. The Susquehannocks, an Iroquoian people, were strategically placed to act as middlemen in early colonial trade on the eastern seaboard. However, this position did not help them avoid attacks by the Iroquois Confederacy and others, and they were essentially wiped out by 1750. This vessel represents a conscious archaism in replacing incised designs with the earlier practice of marking vessels with cord-wrapped paddles or Native textiles. A.M.

Contemporary Works

24/8995 JAR, made by Sara Ayers (Catawba, 1919–2002). Sara Ayers was a strong figure in the resurgence of Catawba pottery-making from the 1950s onward. Catawba potters drew on historic traditions and later added inspirations from thousand-year-old Mississippian pottery traditions. The heads applied to this pot probably represent ancient chiefs and were a trademark element of Sara Ayers's larger works. A.M.

26/1111 SPIDER VASE, made by Lucy Dean Reed (Cherokee, b. 1957). According to Cherokee oral traditions, before the world had fire, the Thunder Beings placed it inside a hollow sycamore tree. After all the other animals had tried and failed to get the fire, Water Spider wove a bowl from her silk and carried the first fire out, thus introducing it to the rest of the world. A.M.

26/5179 9–11, made by Peter B. Jones (Onondaga, b. 1947). Onondaga artist Peter Jones believes that traditional Iroquois pottery was not simply functional but that it also could serve as a mnemonic device to remember historic events and those of everyday life. In this work, he memorializes the events of September 11, 2001, and those who were lost. A.M.

26/5161 CADDOAN HEAD POT, made by Jereldine Redcorn (Caddo/Potawatomi, b. 1939). This vessel is the modern Caddo version of a Mississippian period "head pot"; a similar one was excavated in southwestern Arkansas. Prior to firing her pot, Redcorn burnished its surface with a smooth river pebble and, after it had dried, engraved it with designs typical of Mississippian facial tattooing. After firing, she rubbed red pigment into the crosshatched design. T.E.E.

Endnotes for "Rivers of Interaction"

1. David Brose, "The Woodland Period," in Ancient Art of the American Woodland Indians, 43–92. New York: Harry N. Abrams, Inc. and Detroit Institute of Arts, 1985.

2. The spread of ceramics to Delaware, New York, and Ontario, see James Tuck, "Regional Cultural Development, 3000 to 300 B.C.," in The Northeast, vol. 15, Handbook of North American Indians, ed. B.G. Trigger, 28–43. Washington DC: Smithsonian Institution, 1978. Trade networks and goods, see Brose, "The Woodland Period."

3. James A. Brown, "The Mississippian Period," in Ancient Art of the American Woodland Indians, 93–146. New York: Harry N. Abrams, Inc. and Detroit Institute of Arts, 1985.

4. Vincas P. Steponaitis and Vernon J. Knight Jr., "Moundville Art in Historical and Social Context," in Hero, Hawk, and Open Hand: American Indian Art of the Ancient Midwest and South. Richard F. Townsend and Robert V. Sharp, eds. New Haven: The Art Institute of Chicago and Yale University Press.

5. James A. Brown, "The Mississippian Period."

6. Richard F. Townsend and Robert V. Sharp, eds. Hero, Hawk, and Open Hand: American Indian Art of the Ancient Midwest and South. Chicago: The Art Institute of Chicago and Yale University Press, 2004.

Recommended Readings

Birmingham, Robert A., and Leslie E. Eisenberg. *Indian Mounds of Wisconsin*. Madison: University of Wisconsin Press, 2000.

Brose, David, ed. *Ancient Art of the American Woodland Indians*. New York: Harry N. Abrams, Inc. and Detroit Institute of Arts, 1985.

Fogelson, Raymond D., ed. *The Southeast*, vol. 14, *Handbook of North American Indians*. Washington DC: Smithsonian Institution, 2004.

Power, Susan C. *Early Art of the Southeastern Indians: Feathered Serpents & Winged Beings*. University of Georgia Press, 2004.

Milanich, Jerald T. *Florida's Indians from Ancient Times to the Present*, Gainesville: University of Florida Press, 1998.

Kent, Barry C. *Susquehanna's Indians*. Harrisburg: Pennsylvania Historical And Museum Commission, 1984.

Kraft, Herbert C. *The Lenape-Delaware Indian Heritage, 10,000 B.C. to A.D. 2000*. Lenape Lifeways Inc. 2001.

Snow, Dean R. *The Archaeology of New England*. New York: Academic Press, 1980.

Townsend, Richard F., and Robert V. Sharp, eds. *Hero, Hawk, and Open Hand: American Indian Art of the Ancient Midwest and South*. Chicago: The Art Institute of Chicago and Yale University Press, 2004.

Trigger, Bruce G., ed. *The Northeast*, vol. 15, *Handbook of North American Indians*. Washington DC: Smithsonian Institution, 1978.

MESOAMERICA: THE CULTURAL WELLSPRING OF ANCIENT MEXICO AND CENTRAL AMERICA

PAGE 66

24/3131 OLMEC MALE FIGURE. These solid figures represent the deified children that characterize Olmec cults. F.S.

24/1148 OLMEC RITUAL BOTTLE DEPICTING MYTHOLOGICAL BIRDS. The Olmecs widely traded these black-polished vessels throughout Mesoamerica. The incised designs symbolize the eyes and wings of mythological birds. F.S.

23/4953 OLMEC BOWL. Olmec pottery is characterized by the use of kaolin, which gives it a whitish color, and incised symbolic designs. F.S.

22/9286 PRE-CLASSIC STIRRUP-SPOUT JAR. During the height of development at Tlatilco, terrace and canal agriculture spurred population growth in village communities and a concomitant rise in the diversity of ceramic forms. These may have been used in daily life but are best known from funerary offerings. The most common form was the finely polished red-over-buff stirrup-spout vessel. F.S.

23/5590 PRE-CLASSIC MASK. Red-painted patterns frame the mouth, simulate the eyebrows, and cover the ears of this mask. Pre-Classic figurines show that this kind of mask was attached by its three perforations to a cloth worn over the head during rituals. F.S.

23/9587 PRE-CLASSIC CYLINDER SEAL REPRESENTING TEZCATLIPOCA (GOD OF NIGHT AND WAR) IN JAGUAR DISGUISE. Heavily decorated cylinder seals were very common during the Middle Pre-Classic period in central Mexico. The seals could be rolled in paint to apply designs to textiles, paper, or the human body. This design represents a stylized jaguar recognizable by its claws, tail, and spots. F.S.

PAGE 67

24/1883 XOCHIPALA WOMAN. Xochipala style is characterized by realistic figurines in elegant postures. F.S.

24/7600 CHUPÍCUARO FEMALE FIGURE. The striking facial and body decoration and the cranial deformation seen on this figure suggest that these bodily alterations were important in Chupícuaro society. F.S.

24/7620 CHUPÍCUARO MALE FIGURE. In contrast to other regions of Mesoamerica, the Pre-Classic Chupícuaro tradition has abundant flat male figures. This figure's penis cap highlights his maleness. F.S.

23/1076 CHUPÍCUARO FOUR-LOBED BOWL WITH FACES. Chupícuaro potters often added modeled faces to the walls of ritual vessels such as this one. The eyes—represented by stepped figures—mirror the concentric stepped figures on the other two lobes. F.S.

24/1879 WEST MEXICO FEMALE FIGURINE. This nude woman wears an elegant headdress on which two birds perch. Braids fall down her back. This figure is related to femaleness and earth fertility. F.S.

21/6890 SHAFT TOMBS WARRIOR. This nude male wears armor made of *ixcahuipilli* (cotton fiber) and a wooden helmet. F.S.

PAGE 68

21/122 SHAFT TOMBS MODEL HOUSE. Ancient potters of the Nayarit region depicted everyday life through models such as this. Details of construction are clear: houses were constructed over platforms with stepped levels, while walls were made of logs and ceilings of palm leaves or other fibers. Covered with mud and smoothed, the platforms, walls, and ceilings could be painted with geometric designs. The model also illustrates four women and three men as well as food laid out for their consumption. F.S.

23/2162 SHAFT TOMBS TABLEAU DEPICTING DANCERS AND MUSICIANS. This extraordinary piece likely represents a ritual dance of twelve elaborately dressed dancers. The musicians at the center play drums and *raspadores* (rasps). The men's headdresses are also perforated to make them function as whistles. Depictions of similar dances appear in codices—indigenous documents—from central Mexico. F.S.

RP1535 SHAFT TOMBS MOTHER WITH BABY. The black designs on this figure's face and breasts may represent scarifications or body paint. The rendering of the eyes on the figure is typical of Jalisco stylistic conventions for this period. F.S.

22/5100 SHAFT TOMBS JAR IN THE FORM OF A MAN. Because of his attitude, some scholars suggest that this man is philosophizing. The muscles on his back give this vessel extraordinary realism. Traces of red paint surround his mouth. F.S.

22/5716 SHAFT TOMBS "CLOWN" FIGURE. Seated human figures of this type are popularly called "clowns" because of the protuberances on their heads and the ornaments around their necks. However, these figures probably represent high-status individuals, possibly warriors. The ears on this figure show traces of earspools. F.S.

24/5973 SHAFT TOMBS SCORPION-SHAPED VESSEL. The scorpion is associated with war and symbolizes a star constellation. F.S.

PAGE 69

24/452 SHAFT TOMBS EMACIATED DOG. This animal, with its bony back and phallic character, guided the dead on their travels to the Underworld. F.S.

23/5498 SHAFT TOMBS FUNERARY MASK. Funerary bundles of high-status individuals in western Mexico were wrapped in textiles and topped with modeled clay masks, meant to represent idealized human features rather than specific portraits. The masks typically are polished and include perforations at the ears and the top of the head that allow them to be tied to the bundle. F.S.

23/2276 SHAFT TOMBS MALE FIGURE. Highly stylized Nayarit-style figures are almost caricatures of their subjects. This figure, a mate to the female figure (23/2275), represents a chief-warrior wearing a *máxtlatl* (loincloth) and a short cape and holding an axe. He has a conical headdress, a nose ornament, and multiple earrings. F.S.

23/3868 SHAFT TOMBS MOTHER AND CHILDREN. This group of red figures depicts the mother goddess in the shape of a mountain surrounded by sixteen babies. F.S.

16/6067 TEOTIHUACÁN JAR. The figure represents Huehuetéotl, the Old God or god of fire, with his wrinkled face and few remaining teeth. The use of thin orange ware is characteristic of Teotihuacán ceramics. F.S.

PAGE 70

23/3434 TEOTIHUACÁN JAR. The city of Teotihuacán in the Valley of Mexico held sway over most of central Mexico, and even beyond, and imposed its rain-god cult on neighboring peoples. The spread of this cult is indicated by the excavation of this jar depicting Tláloc with his serpent scepter from the ruins of Monte Albán, the Zapotec capital. F.S.

24/6989 TEOTIHUACÁN PRIEST WEARING A TLÁLOC MASK. This figurine with its Tláloc (rain god) mask and complex feather headdress was made by using appliqué techniques. F.S.

24/3383 TEOTIHUACÁN CYLINDRICAL TRIPOD JAR WITH COVER. Teotihuacán, as a powerful city-state, drew on ceramic ideas from other parts of Mesoamerica and redistributed these through exchange networks. Covered tripod vessels with straight walls were the most popular form for trade. This extraordinary example includes a number of decorative techniques, including polishing, appliqué, and carving. The figure on the cover with ringed eyes and mouth represents the rain god. F.S.

22/9282 TEOTIHUACÁN CYLINDRICAL TRIPOD JAR. Teotihuacán artists sometimes used stucco and fresco—techniques more commonly used to decorate buildings—on their ceramics. After firing, ceramics were covered with a thin stucco layer, which was painted while the stucco was still moist. These designs illustrate feathers surrounding spheres of jade (chalchíhuitl) on a field of red, symbolizing blood. F.S.

24/2975 CLASSIC TEOTIHUACÁN-STYLE WEST MEXICO DOUBLE BOWL. The influence of the Teotihuacán city-state on other Mesoamerican regions is apparent in this fresco-painted double vessel. In western Mexico, specifically Guanajuato and Michoacan, double vessels were built via a tubular basal element. The base of this piece is painted with a scene reminiscent of mural painting where two sacred animals—the jaguar representing Tezcatlipoca and the feathered serpent representing Quetzalcóatl—confront one another. As he is here, Tezcatlipoca is often accompanied by a coyote. F.S.

24/7762 MAYA TRIPOD BOWL DEPICTING A BIRD. Complex iconographic imagery typifies the Maya's famous plates and vases from the Classic period. The bird on this bowl corresponds to a mythological personage named Moan. This piece was painted before firing, and mineral pigments were also applied after firing. F.S.

PAGE 71

24/4089 MAYA CYLINDRICAL RITUAL VASE. The extraordinary figures on this vase represent Maya chiefs or warriors in a procession. One wears a curved headdress and a fan-like feather ornament on his back, and holds a scepter made of cotton with hanging strips. A trophy head—with the hair hanging down—is suspended from his neck. The other two figures wear headdresses in the form of a flower and a fish and carry simpler scepters ornamented with cotton and feathers. F.S.

24/4314 MAYA CYLINDRICAL RITUAL VASE DEPICTING PRIESTS. Cylindrical vessels like these were used in Maya ceremonies dedicated to the gods and in funerary rituals, and these polychrome ceramics are a testament to the abilities of ancient painters. In one scene on this vase, a chief or priest wearing an elegant headdress appears to be playing a musical instrument, while in the other he is accompanied by a trophy head. The upper band represents stylized glyphs from the Maya writing system. F.S.

23/3781 JAINA-STYLE MAYA WHISTLE. Most Jaina-style Maya figurines were musical instruments used in processional ceremonies and funerary rites. This whistle depicts a complexly dressed high-status person wearing a great headdress and a spiral-shaped snail as a pectoral. The figure has traces of Maya blue paint. F.S.

23/8368 JAINA-STYLE MAYA PRIEST. This figure, which has a whistle on its back, wears a feather headdress and band with circular plaques, a máxtlatl (loincloth), and a shell pectoral. His face exhibits elaborate scarification. F.S.

23/2216 JAINA-STYLE MAYA FIGURE OF THE RULER HALACH HUINIK. Basal perforations suggest this figure was carried in ritual processions. It depicts the ruler Halach Huinik, seated on his throne inside a room ornamented with a bird, a human head, two serpent heads in profile, and other animal images. The back part of the object is completely flat, evidence that it was mold-made. F.S.

PAGE 72

23/2573 JAINA-STYLE MAYA DRUNKARD. This man holds a pair of guajes (gourds) and is dressed only in a máxtlatl (loincloth), knotted in the back. He has a beard, and his face is scarified. F.S.

23/2865 JAINA-STYLE MAYA WEAVER. Even among the exquisite figurines created by Maya artists, this figure of a weaver stands out. Thought to represent the Maya goddess Ixchel, she wears a huipil and a bead necklace, and exhibits the cranial deformation common during this period. Realistic details distinguish the waist-loom tied to a tree trunk. An identical figure in the collections of the National Museum of Anthropology in Mexico includes a bird, which suggests that this figure once had the same detail. F.S.

23/9576 CLASSIC CENTRAL VERACRUZ FEMALE-FIGURE RATTLE. These figurines, a variation of the famous Jaina figures, were produced throughout a vast area of the Gulf Coast, from the Maya area to Veracruz. Traces of the original Maya-blue paint depict stepped frets. F.S.

24/3352 CLASSIC FLUTE WITH MONSTER FIGURE. Some Veracruz cultures made flutes with complex decorations and symbolism. This flute has two mouths and the figure surmounting the platform represents a man impersonating a creature that combines the attributes of different animals, including a crocodile head and tail. A reclining woman—made in a separate mold and then applied—lies at the crocodile-man's feet. F.S.

23/4048 CLASSIC FLUTE. All Mesoamerican cultures celebrated feasts and ceremonies with music and dancing, with wind instruments being most common. This object is typical of the Veracruz region and includes a molded human head ornamented by the figure of a bird. F.S.

24/3351 CLASSIC CENTRAL VERACRUZ TROPHY-HEAD VESSEL. Although red-on-buff decoration is associated with Huaxtec traditions, the clay used for this piece and particularly its red paint suggest a central Veracruz origin. The incised facial scarifications give this magnificent figure a serpent-like character. F.S.

PAGE 73

23/6257 REMOJADAS MALE FIGURE HOLDING A BIRD. Remojadas style is characterized by natural, anatomically correct designs, as is very evident in this figure. His face is painted with chapopote (tar). F.S.

24/3599 REMOJADAS SEATED NOBLE OR PRIEST. Remojadas-style figurines are found in several regions of south-central Veracruz. Those of the Huachín region have a soft white painting and fine appliquéd details. This high-status individual is seated on his throne and holds scepters in his hands. F.S.

22/2310 REMOJADAS FEMALE-FIGURE WHISTLE. The elaborate ornament on this woman's head probably represents a net with rounded elements. On her back is a whistle, indicating that this figure was used as a musical instrument during ceremonies. F.S.

22/6374 REMOJADAS WHISTLE DEPICTING WOMEN ON A SWING. This figurine is in the El Faisán style, which is characterized by the use of red paint to depict both clothing and facial and body decoration. One woman has a lock of hair hanging over part of her face, while the other wears a headdress with alternating horizontal and vertical designs. F.S.

PAGE 74

22/9277 REMOJADAS FEMALE FIGURINE HOLDING FAN. This woman wears the typical female costume of a skirt and quexquemitl (smock). The whole figure is painted buff; its mouth is decorated by a pre-firing application of chapopote (tar), and horizontal bands of red paint applied post-firing adorn the skirt. F.S.

23/8555 REMOJADAS PRIEST. This priest wears a long tunic, a headdress with two discs, a complex pectoral necklace, and a mask made of human flesh related to the cult of Xipe Tótec (god of spring and agriculture). He uses a scepter as a cane. F.S.

24/2721 TOTONAC FOOTED BOWL WITH BIRD DESIGN. A very stylish bird is painted on the bottom of this vessel. It is probably a vulture (zopilote), symbolizing a day in the Native calendar related to war. F.S.

23/653 TOTONAC RATTLE-BASE PEDESTAL BOWL DEPICTING A CROUCHING DOG. This vessel has a solar-sacrificial character: solar rays are depicted on its edge, and the dog, symbolizing an offering of war, is penetrated by an arrow. Its base, in the shape of a conical log, functioned as a rattle during ceremonies. F.S.

6/582 PAQUIMÉ VESSEL IN THE FORM OF A WOMAN. The complete nakedness of the figure is related to fertility rites: her hand-to-breast position signifies she is feeding her children. The painted designs on both the front and back of this figurine indicate that Casas Grandes people painted their faces and bodies. F.S.

6/586 PAQUIMÉ VESSEL IN THE FORM OF A WOMAN. This woman's nakedness and open belly are related to maternity. The designs on her belly represent the four directions of the universe. F.S.

23/7067 TARASCAN TRIPOD BOWL WITH RATTLE BASE. The Tarascan Empire extended through much of Michoacan and parts of Guerrero. Tarascan ceramics often had a shiny surface, and polychrome tripod vessels with supports in the shape of human legs were common funerary offerings. The geometric designs resemble those used on textiles of the same period. F.S.

24/7623 TARASCAN PIPE WITH JAGUAR-HEAD RATTLE. Based on images from the Tarascan colonial codex (a form of indigenous chronicle drawn on bark paper) La Relación de Michoacán, Tarascan kings and nobility at the imperial capital of Tzintzuntzan used pipes like these during important ceremonies. F.S.

24/7945 TARASCAN RITUAL JAR WITH SPOUT AND LONG NECK TOPPED BY A RING. Ritual jars like this, found in funerary offering in Tzintzuntzan, the Tarascan capital, and other important cities, illustrate the fantastic creativity of Tarascan artists. F.S.

23/7831 POST-CLASSIC WEST MEXICO FEMALE FIGURE WITH CHARACTERISTICS OF THE MALE XIPE TÓTEC (GOD OF SPRING AND AGRICULTURE). This figure is an unusual female representation of Xipe Tótec (god of spring and agriculture). The impersonator wears the flayed skin of a sacrificial victim, the conical headdress, and the mask of human flesh characteristic of this god. F.S.

15/6338 AZTEC MASK. This mask of Tláloc (the rain god) shows his typical eye rings, rolled nose, and serpent fangs. The two perforations on the mask's upper surface suggest its use as a pendant. F.S.

16/3393 CHOLULA-STYLE AZTEC CYLINDRICAL CUP WITH PEDESTAL BASE. Cholula polychrome ceramics were fired twice: once as plain vessels and again at a lower temperature after application of a thin layer of painted stucco. The painted designs include the heads of two eagles or vultures, representing war, stars, and abstract teeth and eyes. F.S.

23/6187 CHOLULA-STYLE AZTEC MALE FIGURE. This extraordinary figure of Quetzalcóatl (the wind god) combines his usual symbolic attributes of a headdress with long pendants with the conical headdress of Xipe Tótec (god of spring and agriculture) and the red-and-black face painting typical of Tezcatlipoca (god of night). F.S.

23/6188 CHOLULA-STYLE AZTEC FEMALE FIGURE. This figure makes a pair with the wind god figure (23/6187); both were found in the same cave. With her characteristic chapopote (tar) facial painting, she represents the earth's fertility as the corn goddess. In one hand she carries the sun's rays (xicahuaztli). F.S.

4/9692 COATLALPANEC-STYLE AZTEC GLOBULAR DRUM. This vessel, pieced together from a solid upper section set into the lower pierced section, was used as a drum. By varying the level of water, different tones could be produced. The applied head represents that of Xochipilli Macuilxóchitl, the music god. F.S.

24/7783 POST-CLASSIC MAYA CENSER. The city-state of Mayapán dominated the whole Yucatán peninsula during the Post-Classic period. This incense burner depicts Chac, the Maya god of rain. His emerging tongue transforms into two drops of water. F.S.

26/5279 INCENSARIO (CENSER). In Mesoamerican ceremonies, copal—the dried resin of the copal tree—is placed on burning charcoal in an incensario to produce a thick, sweet smoke. When used as incense, copal is called "the food of the gods" and is analogous to the Native North American use of tobacco to carry prayers and thoughts to deities. A.M.

THE SOUTHWESTERN UNITED STATES: CONTINUITY AND CHANGE

Bridging Space and Time

19/4356 ZUNI OLLA (WATER JAR). Mid-nineteenth-century jars can be identified by their rounded bodies and hatched designs. These dancing figures seem to be both parrots with magnificent tails and crests and a row of woman dancers wearing tablita headdresses. B.B.

26/4272 IMPRISONED CLOWN, made by Roxanne Swentzell (Santa Clara, b. 1962). Unlike many of her contemporaries, Swentzell works with commercial clays and fires in an electric kiln, but her connection to her Pueblo heritage is unflinching and unabashed. Her pieces are highly personal—each figure a chapter of her distinguished career. Swentzell uses humor and visual puns to question her own life as well as her culture's.

6/201 TESUQUE DOUBLE-SPOUT PITCHER. Two-colored jars are unique to Tesuque and were made only during the last two decades of the nineteenth century. Water designs on pitchers probably represent a profound prayer for rain. However, we do not know if these bicolor vessels held a special status or use. B.B.

10/6625 ZUNI COOKING POT. Corrugated cooking wares were used continuously throughout the Southwest from A.D. 600 to the early twentieth century. Potters usually made the indented corrugations with a stick or even their fingers. However, on this jar, they were made by adding small pinched coils to the pot's exterior. B.B.

26/4157 BLACK-ON-BLACK JAR, made by Adam Martinez (San Ildefonso, 1903–2000) and Santana Roybal Martinez (Santa Clara, 1909–2002). Adam Martinez was Maria and Julian Martinez's eldest son; Santana Roybal was the niece of Tonita Roybal. Santana learned to make pottery from her mother-in-law, Maria Martinez. When Julian Martinez passed away in 1943, Santana became Maria's potting partner, painting the pots. In the mid-1950s when Maria began working with her son, Popovi Da, Santana worked with her husband to produce beautifully conceived and executed black-on-black wares. B.B.

Continuity, Change, and Creativity

10/9676 HOPI JAR. Although this water storage jar was excavated near Zuni Pueblo, its materials and designs align it with ancestral Hopi, or Sityaki, wares of the same period, confirming the close relationships and movements of people between villages for trade and in times of drought. B.B.

19/4360 HOPI-TEWA GOURD-SHAPED CANTEEN. The potter studied the shape of a gourd to produce a wonderfully functional water canteen with a handle for pouring. B.B.

21/2682 SITYATKI REVIVAL JAR, made by Rachel Nampeyo (Hopi/Tewa, 1903–1985). The famed Hopi potter Nampeyo revived the Sityaki pottery style (A.D. 1325–1600). Rachel Nampeyo worked with her mother and also made her own pots. One of her favorite designs was the "migration" pattern. B.B.

25/8343 JAR, made by Maria Martinez (San Ildefonso, 1887–1980) and Popovi Da (San Ildefonso, 1921–1971). Over her eight-decade career, Martinez worked with her husband, Julian, her daughter-in-law Santana, and her son Popovi. In twenty years working together, she and her son produced some of the best pottery made at the pueblo. The techniques Popovi developed—sgraffito, duotone, sienna slip, gunmetal finish, and inlaid turquoise and heshi—have not yet been replaced by fresh innovations. B.B.

26/4159 SEED JAR, made by Grace Chino (Acoma, 1929–1994). Chino did not rely on a signature design, being guided instead by the balance of her form and painting. She revived and made contemporary the thousand-year-old seed jar form. The modulated sizing of the painted design and the way it covers almost the entire pot accentuate the jar's shape. B.B.

25/5843 MELON BOWL, made by Nancy Youngblood (Santa Clara, b. 1955). Youngblood expresses her artistry by both continuing her community's traditional pottery technologies and pushing their limitations. Before firing this pot, she carved and polished each rib, and after firing, she again polished the vessel to achieve absolute evenness of tone. Youngblood works painstakingly, creating fewer than twenty-five pieces per year. B.B.

Visions of Worlds

19/2701 HOPI-TEWA STORAGE JAR. While the heavy crackly slip of this pot is characteristic of Hopi Polacca Polychrome, its designs are usually associated with Zuni pottery, a late-nineteenth-century reinterpretation of 500-to-800-year-old patterns. B.B.

19/6726 COCHITI FIGURINE. This enraptured singer captures the power of song in the Pueblo world. His Pueblo identity is further defined by the bag slung over his shoulder, his long loose hair, and his vest decorated with corn and water symbols. Pueblo potters have long used their art to incorporate other worlds into their own, thereby making them knowable and allowing the outside and Pueblo worlds to coexist and commingle. B.B.

23/4992 ACOMA OLLA (WATER JAR). The narrowed middle of this jar is unusual but suggests an affinity with canteens or other water containers. The magnificent orange and red zigzag band is usually interpreted as water or a rainbow. Upon this band, deer (rendered in a Zuni style) stand, several alerted to something moving behind them. B.B.

25/9871 *OLLA* (WATER JAR), made by Margaret Tafoya (Santa Clara, 1904–2001). Tafoya, one of the master potters of the twentieth century, was the matriarch of Santa Clara pottery. She defined the potting styles of her pueblo and built its reputation for well-conceived and executed pottery. Her signature style was a well-built and balanced pot, with deep lustrous polishing and an indented bear paw. B.B.

22/7879 ZUNI *OLLA* (WATER JAR). The olla is a metaphor for the balance that Zuni people seek throughout their culture. Zuni potters use crushed pot-sherds for temper to reduce shrinkage of the clay during firing. B.B.

Pueblo Pottery and Change

471 MOGOLLON (TULAROSA) BOWL. This pot combines a textured outer surface with a smooth, polished, and blackened interior. The potter used small coils of clay to build the pot, and achieved the corrugations by not smoothing or sanding the surface. B.B.

5/3861 TEWA STORAGE JAR. Large jars were used to store food, clothes, or other household goods. While this pot exhibits attributes from both the Northern Tewa and southern Keresan pueblos, the thin red line dividing the red base from the white body and the dominant Tewa iconography suggest the Powhoge attribution. B.B.

26/5271 *DINO CUBE*, made by William Pacheco (Santo Domingo, b. 1975). Like many children, Pacheco was fascinated by dinosaurs. In the late 1980s, his uncle encouraged him to paint them on his pottery. As an adult, Pacheco still experiments with his favorite designs, and with his clay, as this slab-built cube shows. But even with dinosaurs on a cube, his work retains the unmistakable hallmarks of Santo Domingo's pottery traditions. B.B.

Figurines

7502 COCHITI SINGING-MAN PITCHER. The functionality of this water pitcher is combined with its whimsicality. The figure's open mouth and uplifted eyes indicate that he is singing. B.B.

7528 TESUQUE DEVIL FIGURE. The crown on this figure suggests it represents a devil. Interestingly, its posture is reminiscent of figures from pre-Columbian Mexico. Many early scholars speculated that Pueblo people were the ancestors of the vanquished Toltecs of central Mexico. Shrewd traders apparently seized on this idea, asking potters to duplicate pre-Columbian figurative pottery traditions. This figure is made of micaceous clay, slipped with red, and painted with plant-based paint. B.B.

6/6819 COCHITI PITCHER DEPICTING A SNAIL (?). Figurative traditions are quite old at Cochiti, with potters often evoking water through their choice of animals. This animal's association with star icons likely was a critical connection, but its meaning is now lost to time. We can, however, imagine that the potter's intention was to make two disparate worlds knowable by bringing them together in one pot. B.B.

6/6820 COCHITI SINGING MAN, CA. 1890. That this man is singing is indicated by his uplifted head and eyes and his raised hands. Realistic birds and water creatures are unusual on figurative pottery. B.B.

11/5015 COCHITI DUCK FIGURE. Symbiosis of form and function is complete in Cochiti figurative pottery traditions. Here we have the poignancy of a water container made in the shape of a water creature. B.B.

16/9763 COCHITI ANIMAL-HUMAN FIGURINE. By combining humans with animals, the familiar with the unfamiliar, this unknown potter brings the unknown outside world into the safer confines of Pueblo culture. B.B.

21/1134 COCHITI ANIMAL-HUMAN FIGURINE. The head of this figure is clearly that of a singing man. However, he stands on four legs and has a small pug tail. The cranes and herons that amble around this pot's sides suggest its use as a water pitcher. B.B.

26/5237 STANDING CLOWN FIGURE, made by Lisa Holt (Cochiti, b. 1980) and Harlan Reano (Santo Domingo, b. 1978). This figure brings together the centuries-old Pueblo practice of reviving pottery traditions with academic research substantiating that late-nineteenth-century Cochiti figures include images of traveling circus clowns. Over the past few decades, interest in single standing figures has grown at Cochiti Pueblo, particularly as a result of Holt's uncle Virgil's work. This young couple has only been making pottery for a few years; he paints the pieces that she builds. B.B.

Canteens

4/742 HOPI-TEWA GOURD-SHAPED CANTEEN. This piece is unusual for its realistic depiction of a gourd. Cut and shaped gourds are used as water dippers, pottery-making tools, and rattles. B.B.

6/6828 ZIA CANTEEN. Single canteens were plugged with a corncob and worn on a belt or bandolier. The flowers and vines evoke well-watered places. B.B.

16/1513 ACOMA CANTEEN. The designs on this canteen are both prayers for rain and expressions of the fertility brought by moisture, as represented by plants, flowers, and corn. A large canteen such as this would probably have been used in a house rather than carried. B.B.

26/5269 CANTEEN. His colleagues say that Begaye is a potter's potter because of his knowledge of materials and techniques. He consistently locates new materials, then uses them in his work to create novel effects, such as the deep green and textured rust-colored surfaces of this canteen. B.B.

Ceramics as Autobiographies

5/3048 ANCESTRAL PUEBLO BOWL. These ducks or cranes appear to carry bird nets filled with humans. Two small holes in the pot's body are a Native repair; a thong laced between them would have held the crack together. The abundance of Red Mesa wares at Chaco Canyon is not yet fully explained, for their clays suggest they were made elsewhere. They were either traded to Chaco or were brought in by visitors to this apparently great cultural/ceremonial center. B.B.

17/5988 *OLLA* (WATER JAR), made by Tsayutitsa (Zuni, ca. 1875–ca. 1955). Tsayutitsa is one of the master potters of the twentieth century, her work unmistakable. Traders and anthropologists asked Tsayutitsa and other Zuni potters to emulate 500-year-old pottery excavated from Hawikuu, an abandoned Zuni town. A brown tempera paint wash further ages the pots. Nonetheless, the uniformity of their chimerical features betrays these pots' intended use—to create a market for a fabricated authenticity. B.B.

19/4337 SAN ILDEFONSO JAR DEPICTING A HUNT. The two men clearly disagreeing with one another and the wounded bear spitting lighting at the hunter, as well as the two animals climbing the tree to escape, all suggest an emotional scene. Men painted these distinctively male narratives, which probably are artistic interpretations of real events. B.B.

24/3196 MIMBRES BOWL. Mimbres pottery has long captured our imagination. Each bowl seems to depict a realistic scene taken from the lives of Mimbres people. But closer examination shows that this painted antelope is transforming, as evidenced by the badger paws on its front legs and its human feet. B.B.

Ceramics as Narratives

12/3843 ZUNI JAR. This jar is unusual: The arms appear on opposite sides of the vessel, and the designs painted on them are typical of pottery made 100 to 400 years earlier. The arm decoration probably represents body painting; tattooing has never been a Pueblo practice. From ca. A.D. 1325 to 1725, Pueblo people used lead-based glazes as paints, rather than as a finishing gloss. B.B.

21/6838 COCHITI STORAGE JAR. This large jar tells a hunting story: deer and antelope move through the pine trees with a mythical hunter in pursuit. B.B.

22/7882 ZUNI *OLLA* (WATER JAR) DEPICTING DEER. This unusual vessel represents either hunting or fertility, the latter suggested by the numbers of deer and fawns. The lack of clearly defined base and neck designs breaks typical painting conventions, as does the use of a continuous pattern instead of panels separated by medallions. B.B.

24/7772 VASE, made by Lucy M. Lewis (Acoma, 1895–1992). This masterpiece won second place at the 1962 New Mexico State Fair. Revival of black-on-white pottery began in the 1870s, culminating in the wholesale copying of older pots. Lewis's use of earlier designs was usually more subtle, for she understood the design iconography well enough to adapt it to a variety of new shapes. B.B.

25/4761 JAR, made by Jody Folwell (Santa Clara, b. 1942). Folwell describes this as an early piece, made when she began to experiment with her now-signature brown clay and slip. She characterized the lizards dancing around it as "playful." When pressed for a more in-depth explanation, she responded, "Why not?" B.B.

25/9870 VASE, made by Tony Da (San Ildefonso, b. 1940). Tony Da is the son of Popovi and Anita Da and the grandson of Maria Martinez. In 1966, he moved into his grandmother's home and began learning from her. His perfecting of techniques he learned from his father—as evidenced in this highly polished jar, with balanced sienna oval, sgraffito deer, and inlaid shell—marks his spectacular career. B.B.

26/5061 *LAND OF ENTRAPMENT*, made by Russell Sanchez (Santa Clara, b. 1966). *Entrapment* is a commentary on the many outside forces that intrude on Pueblo culture, including Christianity and tourism. Some of these, Pueblo people regret, are unavoidable or even needed—thus the sense of entrapment. B.B.

26/5062 *OLLA* (WATER JAR), made by Lois Gutierrez de la Cruz (Pojoaque, b. 1949). Lois Gutierrez de la Cruz builds narratives through the scenes she paints on her pots; her revival of the seventeenth-century Tewa form of tall-necked, wide-shouldered ollas; and her continual experimentation with different clays to produce the colors on her vessels. B.B.

26/4621 *OSAMA KEN-BARBIE*, made by Susan Folwell (Santa Clara, b. 1970) and Franzie Weldgen (b. 1972). Potters have always told us who they are and their concerns and aspirations for the world they live in. We are used to seeing pots that tell a Puebloan story, but what about other influences on modern Pueblo society? In this satirical piece, a traditionally trained potter teamed with a non-Native cartoonist to express her worries—and her proposed solution to the United States' war on terrorism. B.B.

26/5249 *STICKBALL*, made by Diego Romero (Cochiti, b. 1964). Raised in Berkeley, California, Romero studied at the Institute of American Indian Arts and the Otis Art Institute and received his MFA from UCLA; he now lives in Oklahoma with his wife, Lisa Tiger, and their new baby. Drawing on ancient Southwest ceramic narrative traditions and the legacy of his father, a traditional Cochiti painter, Romero uses this autobiographical piece to recognize the traditions of his new family and home. B.B.

PAGE 84

Plates

26/4174 PLATE, made by Christine McHorse (Navajo, b. 1949). Pushing the limits of both technology and materials, McHorse's pottery melds varying influences—polished micaceous clay of her husband's Taos Pueblo traditions and pine-pitch glazing and fire clouds of her Navajo heritage. McHorse makes both functional and sculptural vessels that combine modern and traditional forms with her own sinuously organic shapes. She is also a silversmith and casts some of her sculptures in bronze. B.B.

26/4282 PLATE, made by Margaret Tafoya (Santa Clara, 1904–2001). Margaret Tafoya is the matriarch of a distinguished potting family, which now boasts four generations of potters. She learned to pot from her mother, Sara Fina Tafoya, one of the best potters of her generation. Pottery-making is learned by observation in the pueblo, rather than by explicit teaching. B.B.

26/5270 TILE MASKS, made by Nora Naranjo-Morse (Santa Clara, b. 1953). Naranjo-Morse originally made these tiles for an exhibition of masks at a Santa Fe gallery. A sculptor, filmmaker, published poet, and installation artist, she began her distinguished career selling pottery under the Portal at the Palace of the Governors in Santa Fe. B.B.

24/7564 BLACK-ON-BLACK PLATE, made by Tonita Roybal (San Ildefonso, 1892–1945) and Juan Cruz Roybal (San Ildefonso, 1896–1990). Most ceramics of the early- to mid-twentieth century were made by women and painted by men. Tonita Roybal molded and painted her own pots following her first husband's death in 1913, but she signed this work "Tonita and Juan," indicating that her second husband painted it. The choice and arrangement of ancient Pueblo symbols give the plate an "art deco" sensibility. B.B.

25/8830 PLATE, made by Maria Martinez (San Ildefonso, 1887–1980) and Popovi Da (San Ildefonso, 1921–1971). While Maria Martinez first learned to make polychrome pottery, and created polychrome masterpieces with her husband, by the 1930s her new black-on-black style largely supplanted polychromes at San Ildefonso. The balance of four panels and the painterly quality of this elegant plate, created by a mother-and-son team, were key impetuses for the brief revival of San Ildefonso polychrome wares in the 1960s. B.B.

26/4234 BLACK-ON-BLACK PLATE, made by Maria Martinez (San Ildefonso, 1887–1980) and Julian Martinez, 1879–1943). When Maria built this piece and Julian painted it, matte painting on black lustrous pottery was only ten years old, having been developed by this husband-and-wife team in the winter of 1919–20. By 1930, "two-blacks" had overtaken all other San Ildefonso pottery styles. Depictions of the water serpent, or Avanyu, encircling this plate date back 700 years in southwestern rock art. In the late 1800s, the Avanyu appears on certain types of water bowls made for Pueblo use only. Within the context of developing an economic vehicle for the survival of Pueblo people, Julian began painting the Avanyu on pottery specifically made for non-Pueblo people. B.B.

PAGE 85

Storage Jars

16/5876 SANTO DOMINGO STORAGE JAR. Pueblo potters intentionally make large storage jars with thick walls and heavy bottoms to withstand use and protect their contents. Present-day potters alternatively interpret this design as flowers and loaves of bread. B.B.

5025 ANCESTRAL PUEBLO STORAGE OR WATER JAR. The pattern on this jar suggests small individual kernels of corn, as well as flowers. Ancestral Pueblo people cultivated corn, beans, and squash. B.B.

11/5049 STORAGE JAR, made by Florentino Montoya (San Ildefonso, 1862–1919) and Martina Montoya (Cochiti and San Ildefonso, 1857–1917). This jar is attributed to the Montoyas on the basis of its shape, the slightly outward-curving neck, the distinctive rim motifs, the use of motifs inside motifs, and the horizontal placement of normally vertical designs. These potters had close ties to Cochiti Pueblo, where they moved in 1905. Their use of Cochiti white slip eventually influenced San Ildefonso potters to adopt this technique. B.B.

Work Bowls

5/1087 ACOMA DOUGH BOWL. Pueblo women used large bowls for mixing dough and allowing it to rise. Though made at Acoma, this piece was collected in Isleta Pueblo by anthropologist Jesse Nusbaum. Pottery was a common trade item among the pueblos. B.B.

23/2472 SANTO DOMINGO DOUGH BOWL. Even bowls made for hard use—mixing and kneading bread dough—were beautifully modeled and decorated. The Spanish brought wheat and the beehive-shaped horno ovens used to bake bread to the Pueblo villages. B.B.

PAGE 86

Water Jars

1/7841 LAGUNA *OLLA* (WATER JAR). After filling this large jar with water at a cistern or river, a woman would walk home balancing the pot on her head. The plant designs covering this jar are all prayers for moisture. Laguna and neighboring Acoma potters revived indigenous black-on-white pottery during the second half of the nineteenth century. B.B.

8/7674 ACOMA DOUBLE *OLLA* (WATER JAR). The antiquity of this vessel is indicated by its double bulbous form and its broad, singularly painted designs. Nearby pueblos use the double form for canteens or bird-effigy jars. B.B.

19/7294 SAN ILDEFONSO *OLLA* (WATER JAR), made by Tonita Roybal (San Ildefonso, 1892–1945); painting attributed to Crescencio Martinez (San Ildefonso, 1879–1918). Roybal's signature revival of the seventeenth-century Tewa Polychrome water-jar shape, as well as her skill in making well-proportioned and polished pots, suggests attribution of this olla to her. Martinez's even hand and symmetrical designs are evident in the jar's shoulder and body designs. B.B.

20/8459 SANTA CLARA RAINBOW JAR OR *OLLA* (WATER JAR). High polished blackware was first described in 1880 at Santa Clara Pueblo. Smothering the open kiln fire carbonizes the ceramic surface; if the fire is not smothered, the pot fires red. These wares are the direct descendants of a pottery style known as Kapo blackware that dates from ca. A.D. 1550. B.B.